# THE LOVE OF ELEPHANTS

# THE LOVE OF ELEPHANTS

## NEIL MURRAY

OCTOPUS

First published 1976 by
Octopus Books Limited
59 Grosvenor Street, London W1

ISBN 0 7064 0515 3

Produced by Mandarin Publishers Limited
22A Westlands Road, Quarry Bay,
Hong Kong

Printed in Hong Kong

# CONTENTS

# PREHISTORIC ELEPHANTS

 The two living elephant species— *Loxodonta africana* in Africa and *Elephas maximus* in Asia—are the only surviving descendants of an immense group of species which for many millions of years were the dominant animals on earth. The prehistoric elephants maintained their ascendancy until the Pleistocene, the period of about two and a half million years immediately preceding the emergence of modern man. This was a time of unprecedented faunal prosperity when the whole world was the unencumbered domain of wild animals. In variety as well as sheer numbers, wildlife had by then reached the culmination of many millions of years of evolution, filling every available ecological niche on land and sea and in the air.

By the time of the great flowering of the Pleistocene, the Proboscidea—the order of mammals which includes the elephants—had reached a peak of development, appearing in a remarkable number of types and spreading virtually all over the world. Almost every continent had its quota. But the beginnings of this fascinating order of mammals extend back infinitely farther into the past, reaching over periods of time measured in figures so astronomical that they are almost too difficult to comprehend.

Remains of the earliest proboscidean yet discovered were found at Lake Moeris in the

**Left: A life-like model of the woolly mammoth showing the scythe-like tusks, probably used for sweeping snow from the underlying vegetation.**

**Above: A reconstruction of an imperial mammoth at the famous Rancho la Brea tarpits, near Los Angeles, which yielded the fossilized remains of a great many Pleistocene animals.**

A chart of the evolution of the Proboscidea from the ancestral *Moeritherium*
to the two living species, seen against
the geological time scale. The four
families which together make up this
order of mammals are each represented
by one or two 'typical' species. There
were, of course, many more, totalling
altogether about 300 species.

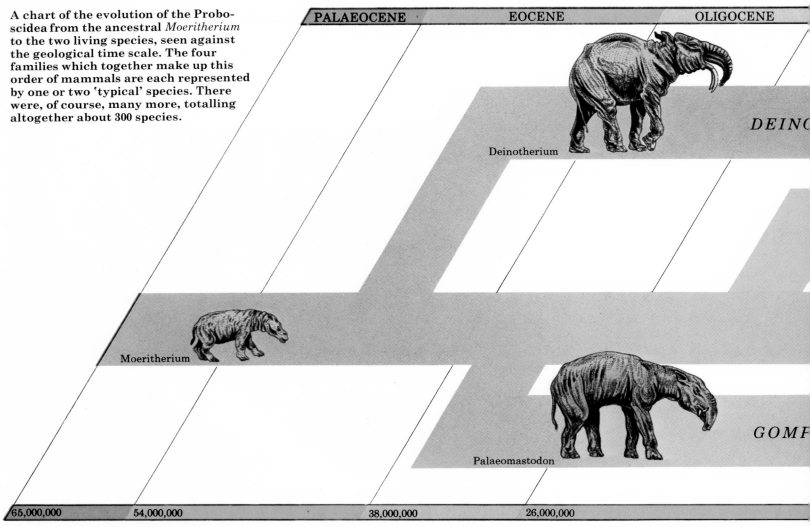

Deinotherium

DEINO

Moeritherium

Palaeomastodon

GOMP

65,000,000    54,000,000    38,000,000    26,000,000

Egyptian province of Fayum, where it first
appeared during the Palaeocene, some 65–54
million years ago. This animal–named
*Moeritherium* after the lake by which it was
found–bore little resemblance to the modern
elephant. It was a pig-sized animal with ears
and eyes positioned high on its head, features
suggesting that it may have looked more like
a pygmy hippopotamus than an elephant.
But, although it possessed no trunk, the
structure of its skull and teeth is unmistak-
ably elephantine: in particular it had rudi-
mentary tusks in both its upper and lower
jaws. These and other physical features, for
reasons that will be explained later, suggest
that the moerithere lived in and around
swamps, marshlands and rivers.

From these beginnings the ancestral
elephants gradually spread farther and
farther from their centre of origin. This
process, known as 'adaptive radiation', is
stimulated by the growth of population and
consequent shortage of food and living space
forcing groups of animals to move outwards
from the centre into areas where competition
is less severe.

In this way, and over a period of time so
immense that it has to be seen against the
perspective of the geological time scale,
the proboscideans eventually populated not
only the whole of Africa and much of
Eurasia but moved into North America as
well–North America and Eurasia being at
that time joined together across what is now
the Bering Strait. The colonization of new
areas meant that species had to adapt to meet
altered environmental and climatic conditions which led, through the normal processes of evolution, to the creation of new
types of animals.

The extraordinary adaptability of the
proboscideans was shown by their successful
colonization not only of every continent
except Australia and Antarctica, but of
almost every conceivable type of habitat.
The territories they moved to ranged from
temperate regions enveloped in snow for part
of each year to the scorching sunshine of the
tropics, from open grasslands to dense forest,
and from wetlands to semi-arid zones. By the
beginning of the Miocene–about 26 million
years ago–the proboscideans had evolved
into an astonishing variety of types, some of
almost unbelievably grotesque
appearance.

The multitude of distinctive types,
numbering altogether about 300 separate
species, can be condensed into four principal
groupings: the Deinotheriidae, the Gompho-
theriidae, the Mastodontiidae, and the
Elephantidae.

*Deinotherium*–which first appeared in the
Eocene, about 54–38 million years ago–was
almost the size of a present-day elephant. It
had a well-developed trunk, but its tusks
sprouted from the lower jaw, curling downwards and with the tips pointing backwards.
The precise use of these unconventional
tusks is uncertain. Many theories have been
put forward, some very fanciful. The most
likely explanation is that they were used to
root up underwater vegetation, rather as a
walrus uses its tusks to root on the seabed for
molluscs. The possession of a trunk gave the
deinothere two great advantages: it was a
highly flexible and mobile limb, of tremendous
help in feeding, and it also enabled the animal
to breathe without having to withdraw its
muzzle from the water. This could help to
explain how the elephant first came to

acquire its trunk. However that may be, the
deinotheres lived for about 50 million years.
They became extinct in Eurasia during the
Pliocene (7–2½ million years ago), but
survived in Africa into the Pleistocene.

The second group, the gomphotheres,
inhabited Africa, Eurasia and North and
South America. They flourished from the
Lower Oligocene–about 38 million years ago
–until well into historical times, clinging to
existence until as recently as the early part
of the Christian era. They were a diverse
group, ranging in height from about 3–10 feet
(0·9–3 metres), including several types
characterized by a relatively long head and
neck and highly specialized jaws.

*Phiomia* and *Palaeomastodon*, among the
earliest members of this group, each had a
pair of short tusks in both the upper and
lower jaws. The elongated lower jaw was
further extended by the arrangement of the
tusks, which curved round to make a shovel-
like protuberance. Whether or not these
animals had crude trunks is uncertain.
Another genus, *Trilophodon*, had an even
more elongated lower jaw, also extended by
a pair of curiously flattened tusks. Its upper
tusks were longer and more conventionally
shaped.

One of the later members of this group,
*Amebelodon*, which lived in the Miocene, had
a pair of tusks 4 feet (1·2 metres) long in its
lower jaw. The effect of these flattened close-
set tusks was to convert the already long jaw
into a large scoop. This suggests that the
animal lived in wetlands, where it fed by
grasping clumps of aquatic vegetation with
its trunk, at the same time using its pro-
truding tusks to sever the stems or roots
before shovelling the food into its mouth.

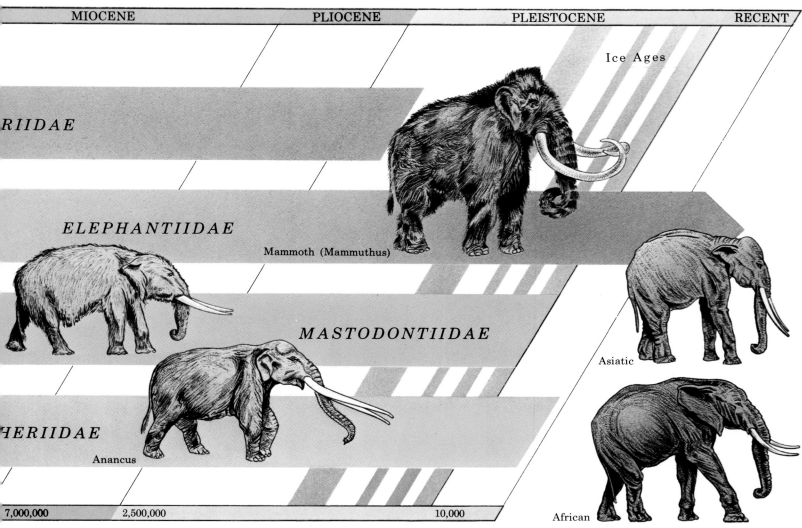

Ice Ages

RIIDAE

ELEPHANTIIDAE

Mammoth (Mammuthus)

MASTODONTIIDAE

Asiatic

HERIIDAE

Anancus

African

7,000,000      2,500,000                                              10,000

The jaw development of other genera in this group went to the opposite extreme. The lower jaw of the Eurasian *Anancus*, for example, was greatly foreshortened, giving it the appearance of being undershot; in contrast, its upper jaw was equipped with a pair of tusks of such unusual length that they were almost three-quarters as long as the animal itself.

While the gomphotheres were evolving in this bizarre manner, the mastodons were developing along somewhat different lines. Mastodons were about the same size as modern elephants but of much more massive build. Although its tooth structure was very different from that of modern elephants, the mastodon's head showed the similar features of a flattened forehead rising to a prominently domed crown, large curved tusks in the upper jaw, and a well-developed trunk. Unlike modern elephants, however, its body was covered with hair.

The wealth of fossil remains discovered in North America tends to give one the impression that the mastodons were exclusive to the New World. In fact they evolved in Eurasia during the Lower Miocene before spreading into Africa and North America. Much later–about two million years ago– when the Isthmus of Panama rose from the ocean floor to link the northern and southern continents of America, which until then had been separated by the sea, there was a two-way inter-continental migration. Among the invaders moving into the hitherto unchallenged domain of the ancient fauna of South America–which for 70 million years had evolved in isolation–were the mastodons. They spread through much of South America, from the grasslands of Argentina

to the Andean highlands of Peru. The mastodons were on earth for about 25 million years, and they are believed to have survived until after the arrival of early man in North America. They remained the dominant group of proboscideans until the beginning of the Pleistocene, when they began to be superseded by the true elephants as we know them today.

The size and strength of the prehistoric elephants were matched by the power of the predators which were their natural enemies, for this was an age of giants. Sabre-toothed cats and tigers, equipped with enormously long fangs and massive forepaws, were well able to kill elephants. Equally formidable was the gigantic dire wolf, an animal much larger than the modern wolf, which hunted in well-regulated packs, killing with ruthless efficiency.

However, not all the prehistoric elephants were of prodigious size. The southerly advances of successive glaciations forced the straight-tusked elephants to move farther south and colonize the Mediterranean region. During the inter-glacials–the warm periods between glaciations–rising water levels isolated the Mediterranean islands, leaving groups of elephants, along with other species, marooned on the islands of Malta, Crete and Cyprus. This restricted habitat resulted in the evolution of a series of dwarf forms of elephant, no larger than Shetland ponies.

The last of the four main proboscidean groupings is the Elephantidae. Members of this group are characterized by an enlarged skull, shorter jaws, and tusks in the upper jaw only. Tusk development in some species is spectacular.

Evolving from *Stegolophodon*–through which it was linked with the mastodons– this group arose during the Miocene, reaching its climax during the Pleistocene. It includes not only the true elephants, which began to make their appearance in the early Pleistocene, and their extinct forebears, but also the mammoths.

The mammoths are undoubtedly the best known of the extinct elephants. Several discoveries of mammoth remains have been made, including complete carcasses so thoroughly deep-frozen in the Siberian permafrost that every detail of the animal's anatomy has been perfectly preserved.

The mammoths, of which there are a number of distinctive species, are related to the modern Asiatic elephant, although they differ from it in a number of important respects. Their relationship with the living Asiatic elephant is, however, closer than the relationship of the Asiatic with the African elephant, for the two living types of elephants we know today are descended from different ancestral stock.

From an examination of tooth structure, palaeontologists can distinguish between animals which browse on leaves, twigs and shoots and must therefore live in woodlands, and grazing animals which because they feed on grass are creatures of the open savannahs. Their teeth identify the straight-tusked mastodons as forest-dwellers whereas the mammoths were essentially grass-eaters, which explains why they chose to live on the Eurasian steppes and the prairielands of North and Central America.

Although size varied greatly according to species, mammoths were generally speaking large animals–substantially larger than the

**Right: An artist's impression of a pre-historic mammoth hunt.**

**Opposite: Stone Age hunters attacking a mammoth in a pitfall (game pit).**

present-day African elephant, the larger of the two remaining species. The so-called imperial mammoth, *Mammuthus imperator*, for instance, had a shoulder height of more than 14 feet (4·2 metres), compared with 11–12 feet (3·3–3·6 metres) for the largest living African elephant. But the imperial mammoth was a giant even among mammoths. By contrast the woolly mammoth, *M. primigenius*, to give but one example, was about the same size as the Asiatic elephant. Although it stood about as high at the shoulder as the Asiatic elephant, the woolly mammoth was shorter in the body; the combination of a pronounced peak to the crown of its head, a prominent shoulder hump, and relatively short hindquarters gave its back a noticeable downward slope.

While the imperial mammoth flourished on the sunny prairielands of the southern United States and Mexico, the woolly mammoth had to adapt itself to infinitely more exacting conditions, for it lived during the Ice Age when the northern parts of Eurasia and North America were under a pall of perpetual ice and snow. The woolly mammoth's physical modifications for life on the edge of the ice sheet included smaller ears, which helped to reduce loss of body heat, and a hide which even by elephantine standards was very thick. The entire body was covered with hair: the dense undercoat was about 1 inch (25 millimetres) in length, but the hair on the flanks and shoulders formed a thick mane up to 20 inches (500 millimetres) long – not unlike the long shaggy coat of the wild yak, and for the same purpose of protecting the animal's underparts from the bitter cold.

Tufts of long hair also protruded from the woolly mammoth's unusually bulbous forehead. This swollen brow held a reserve supply of fat on which the animal could draw when food was scarce: the shoulder hump may have served the same purpose. A layer of fat more than 3 inches (76 millimetres) thick was also stored beneath the skin in the same way, and for the same reason, that a whale is enveloped in a layer of blubber. The woolly mammoth's teeth were highly specialized to deal with the coarse vegetation on which it lived. Its tusks were exceptionally long – up to 15 feet (4·5 metres) or more – extending outwards and downwards before describing a huge arc with the tips almost meeting in front of the face. These strangely shaped

tusks were probably used like twin scythes to sweep aside the snow and expose the underlying vegetation.

The woolly mammoth did not become extinct until about 10,000 years ago. It was therefore contemporary with early man, and its unmistakable image can be seen in a number of cave paintings. To Stone Age man the mammoth and the elephant were valuable sources of food, and their tusks and bones could be turned into weapons and implements.

Early man sometimes indulged in hunting on a large scale as, for example, when an entire herd was ringed by fire or manoeuvred into stampeding over a cliff. But although early man was essentially a predator, and an efficient one at that, there is no reason to suppose that he had any incentive to kill other than to satisfy his own immediate physical requirements.

Why did the prehistoric elephants decline so drastically that all but two species became extinct? Neolithic man may, to be sure, have accelerated the decline of certain species, which for quite different reasons were already well on the way to extinction, by wiping out the last remnants. But to suggest, as a number of authors have done, that 'over-kill' by man can account for the great Pleistocene extinctions appears to be an altogether untenable assertion. For how could our Neolithic ancestors, relatively sparse on the ground, armed only with crude weapons and interested in killing only for the pot, wipe out entire species when Africa south of the Sahara retained a fauna of Pleistocene opulence right down to the arrival of Western man and the introduction of sophisticated weapons? To take another contemporary example, the spectacular herds of bison and pronghorn antelope inhabiting the Great Plains of North America were well able to withstand the pressures of Amerindian hunting – pressures which can hardly have been less severe than those exerted by Neolithic man. Despite heavy and continuous hunting, the American bison flourished; not until the latter part of the nineteenth century, when the declared policy of the United States government was systematically to destroy the animal on which the survival of the Amerindian depended, was it practically exterminated.

Extinction is an integral part of the

evolutionary process: climatic or environmental change, inability to adapt, excessive competition, over-specialization, biological senility, or perhaps some natural disaster are among the causes of natural extinctions. As one species declines or disappears, another rises to take its place, to fill its vacant niche. This has been the ceaseless pattern since the beginnings of life on earth.

But this held true only until the emergence of civilized man: present-day extinctions are in a very different category, for the growing impact of modern man has altogether disrupted the age-old natural pattern. Extinction by human agency is entirely distinct from the natural process, for the simple reason that instead of being a step along the evolutionary way it becomes no more than a dead end.

Today there is a frightening situation of acute over-kill, fostered by the growing multitude of land-hungry and meat-hungry people in the emergent nations of Africa and Asia who, quick to imitate and adopt Western ways, kill less for the pot than for commercial gain. At the same time increasing human populations are occupying or modifying the natural habitats on which the survival of wildlife ultimately depends.

To a greater or lesser extent, these factors affect every living species. The extent to which they have affected the elephants will become apparent in the course of this book.

# THE LIVING ELEPHANTS

Of the large number of different types of proboscideans which at one time almost dominated the earth, only two remain: the African elephant *Loxodonta africana*, inhabiting Africa south of the Sahara, and the Asiatic elephant *Elephas maximus* which is found from India and Ceylon through Burma, Thailand and Malaysia to Sumatra. It also occurs in Borneo, but there is uncertainty whether it has always lived there or whether it was introduced by man.

Some authorities consider that a third type, the African forest elephant (*L.a. cyclotis*), inhabiting the dense tropical rain forests centred on the Congo Basin, is sufficiently distinctive to qualify as a separate species, but the trend of current thinking is to regard it as no more than a subspecies. This diminutive form is nonetheless very distinctive, differing noticeably from the bush elephant. The forest elephant is substantially smaller, standing no more than 8–9 feet (2·4–2·7 metres) at the shoulder – only about two-thirds the height of the bush elephant. Its ears are relatively smaller and more rounded; its tusks thinner, less curved, and tending to point towards the ground rather than forwards. Curiously enough, the skin of the African forest elephant resembles the smooth skin of the Asiatic elephant more closely than that of the African bush elephant. Many other forms of modern elephant have been described, but most are insufficiently differentiated to justify taxonomic separation.

Although the two living species have much in common, they differ substantially, in temperament as well as in physique. The Asiatic elephant is the smaller of the two, adult males standing only about 8–10 feet

**Left: An African elephant strides purposefully to water.**

**Above: Resting beneath a candelabra euphorbia.**

(2·4–3 metres) at the shoulder, compared with the African elephant's height of 10–11 feet (3–3·3 metres) and weight of up to 6 tons (tonnes). The females of both species are smaller than the males; the maximum weight of the African female is 4 tons (tonnes).

One conspicuous physical difference is in the size of the ears, those of the African elephant being much larger, both in actual dimensions and also relative to the animal's overall size. The forehead of the African species is flattened, that of the Asiatic noticeably protrusive; the African elephant's back is hollow, the Asiatic's curves upwards. The skin of the Asiatic elephant is smooth and covered with white or pink depigmentation spots like large freckles which become increasingly numerous with age; the African elephant's skin is far coarser and lacks the 'blotchy' appearance so characteristic of the Asiatic. The trunks of the two species also differ: whereas the African elephant has two finger-like projections on the tip of its trunk, the Asiatic has only one projection.

Tusk differences are very marked: not only are those of the Asiatic species much smaller, Asiatic females are commonly tuskless (or, more accurately, the tusks are so small that they do not protrude beyond the lips), as indeed are a great many bulls: an estimated 90 per cent of Ceylonese elephants are said to be without tusks. The African elephant, on the other hand, almost invariably possesses tusks in both sexes. Tusklessness in the Asiatic elephant may result from persistent killing of tuskers for their ivory: as tusklessness is believed to be a hereditary factor, the continual slaughter of tuskers has resulted in the tuskless strain becoming predominant.

Apart from these physical characteristics, temperaments also differ widely. The Asiatic elephant has been domesticated for centuries, but attempts at schooling the African species have had only limited success. Although normally of a more placid disposition, the adult male Asiatic elephant has periodical bouts of 'musth', when its temporal glands – situated between the eye and the ear – become enlarged and exude an oily substance. When in 'musth' an elephant usually becomes bad-tempered to the point of being dangerous, though not all elephants become wildly excitable when in 'musth': some react in exactly the opposite manner, becoming dull and lethargic. Strange to say, although 'musth' has been a well-known condition since Asiatic elephants were first domesticated, its precise significance remains something of a mystery. What is certain, however, is that when a domesticated elephant is in 'musth' special precautions must be taken to prevent it running amok. The African elephant – of both sexes – is also subject to 'musth' from an early age but, as far as can be judged, it appears to manifest itself in a less violent form.

Of all the animals that have ever lived the elephant ranks among the most successful, so successful in fact that were it not for man the elephant might be the most dominant animal on earth. Perhaps Sir Frank Fraser Darling, the eminent British ecologist, had this in mind when he commented: 'Watching the elephants one was conscious afresh that no other animal has such a wide and varied range: no other animal can occupy so many habitats and it is no wonder the elephant is still the most thriving and resurgent species in much of Africa.'

The elephant's success – in a situation where failure exacts the supreme penalty of extinction – is attributable to its high level of intelligence, its efficiency in exploiting its habitat, its adaptability, and its power of collective action deriving from its well-ordered social organization.

The elephant's success is also partly attributable to its remarkable physique. Vast size in itself confers no overwhelming advantage in nature, as can be seen from the long list of extinct dinosaurs and other gigantic creatures which once roamed the earth. Indeed, mere bulk can be a positive disadvantage, both from the standpoint of hiding from enemies and of the huge intake of food required to sustain it – a problem that can be crucial during drought or other times of scarcity.

An interesting theory put forward by Toni Harthoorn – the distinguished veterinarian whose pioneer work on immobilizing wild animals has made a major contribution to conserving African wildlife – goes further than this: he suggests that bulk may have been a factor in the great Pleistocene extinctions. He postulates that species may have died out as the result of a cumulative deficiency of trace elements – attributable perhaps to altered climatic conditions – a phenomenon that would probably have a more pronounced effect on large animals requiring a bulky diet.

Whatever the truth of this theory, the elephant has been extraordinarily successful in turning its gargantuan size to advantage.

For its strength is commensurate with its bulk: it is by far the most powerful living land animal. The elephant's great strength was brought home to me while game watching in a forest clearing in Kenya. A bad-tempered rhinoceros was occupying a salt-lick near a waterhole. Any animal attempting to come near was promptly seen off; even a small group of elephants emerging from the forest was not permitted to approach. The group of elephants made several attempts, only to be turned away by furious charges, but after this had happened several times, the largest elephant evidently decided that the matter had gone far enough. The next charge failed to intimidate him: he simply stood his ground and as the rhino, head lowered and snorting like a steam engine, turned aside at the last moment, the elephant, judging his timing to perfection, threw his trunk around the rhino's body and, in the twinkling of an eye, flipped the startled animal off its feet.

Despite its prodigious size, one of the elephant's remarkable characteristics is its ability to move almost noiselessly, the pads on the soles of its feet seeming to cushion the sound. From her riverside hide in the Manyara National Park, Oria Douglas-Hamilton, co-author of *Among the Elephants*, once spent an entire day without seeing a single elephant. 'Then suddenly the whole river bed was covered with snorting, rumbling elephants . . . none of us had heard them come. There must have been about one hundred. . . .'

The thickness of the elephant's hide is in keeping with its size but, although thick-skinned, the elephant's body is only sparsely covered with hair. The animal counters this by frequent immersion in water, rounding off its ablutions with a coating of mud applied with its trunk, followed by a good dusting. This not only helps to control skin parasites and to clean and cool the body, it also alleviates the persistent attacks of hordes of flies and other biting insects.

Water is a vital factor in the life of the elephant. Not only must it drink at comparatively frequent intervals (30 gallons (136 litres) or more is the normal daily intake), it must also immerse itself. When water is scarce elephants may have to be content with a wallow or shower, but whenever possible they prefer to indulge in a full-scale bath.

**Left: Egrets frequently associate with elephants. The association is mutually beneficial. The birds feed on the insects kicked up by the elephants and warn the elephants of possible danger.**

**Right: An African elephant plucking vegetation with its trunk.**

Anyone who has watched wild elephants bathing can be left in no doubt that they revel in it. The presence of water seldom fails to produce an air of excitement among the herd, particularly among the calves. Water seems to hold as compelling an attraction for them as it does for small boys: they find it irresistible. One of the finest natural observation posts that I know is Mudanda Rock, a long whale-shaped granite outcrop in Kenya's Tsavo National Park. From the summit one looks down on a large pool where seepage from the base of the rock has filled a natural depression with near-permanent water. The top of the rock is an unrivalled vantage point from which to watch elephants without them knowing that you are there.

During the dry season herds trek from miles around to drink and bathe at Mudanda. As if at an appointed time small groups – many of them as red as the soil with which they last dusted themselves – converge from different directions to mingle at the water's edge. Except for the few designated sentries keeping watch on the approaches, the mood of each group perceptibly changes as it reaches the water. All at once the tension, the straining of senses which normally emanates from the herd like an electric current, is relaxed. As one individual elephant after another dips its trunk or takes its first step into the water, it seems to cast aside its nervousness and be at ease.

And how they enjoy it! The more mature animals first slake their thirst, standing at the edge of the pool and sucking up trunkfuls of water before squirting it into their mouths. After that essential preliminary they wade into deeper water, trunks waving like writhing cobras as they shower water over their backs with almost unseemly abandon. This horseplay progresses through splashing and sousing, before culminating in total immersion, the animal sometimes rolling over and disappearing from view, leaving only the tip of its trunk peeping above the surface like an animated schnorkel.

But however evident the elation of the adults, it is surpassed by the uninhibited delight of the younger members of the herd. They pause from splashing and romping to climb with squeals of pleasure on each other's backs, becoming as abandoned as children at the seaside, in the process often behaving so exuberantly as to earn a hearty slap from an outraged adult's trunk.

Elephants are so much at home in the water that they are naturally competent swimmers. George P. Sanderson, a nineteenth-century authority on Indian wildlife,

describes how in 1875 a batch of 79 Asiatic elephants was sent from Dacca to Barrack-pur near Calcutta by way of the Ganges and several of its large tidal branches: 'In the longest swim they were six hours without touching the bottom; after a rest on a sand-bank, they completed the swim in three more; not one was lost. I have heard of more remarkable swims than this.'

Elephants' ears are equipped with an intricate network of blood vessels running close to the surface, which have an important function in regulating the animal's body temperature. Harthoorn describes the African elephant's ear as 'a gigantic cooling organ. Richly supplied with great blood vessels, it possesses shunts between the arterial and venous systems that allow the blood to flow through at tremendous speed while being cooled by the flapping motion so

characteristic of peaceful elephants.'

The enormous size of these cooling organs can be appreciated from the measurements recorded by Selous, the great hunter-naturalist, who gives the dimensions of an ear from an elephant which stood 10 feet 4 inches (3·2 metres) at the shoulder as 5 feet 6½ inches (1·7 metres) long and 3 feet 3 inches (1 metre) broad; another with a shoulder height of 10 feet (3 metres) had ears which were 5 feet 5 inches (1·6 metres) long and 3 feet 3 inches (1 metre) broad.

If an elephant becomes hot, it will cool itself by spraying water over its head and ears. If chased or harried it sometimes obtains water for this purpose by thrusting its trunk down its own throat and drawing water from its stomach. Although hunters and others had for many years reported this strange happening, it was considered so im-

probable that those who claimed to have seen it were discounted for having too lively an imagination. More recently, however, it has been confirmed by a number of authoritative observers. For instance, in the vicinity of the Kidepo River in Uganda, Bruce Kinloch, at that time Chief Game Warden of Uganda, saw elephants which had been wounded by a party of Karamojong warriors pushing their trunks down their own throats while still on the run and squirting the liquid over their heads, ears and shoulders.

The need to regulate body temperature helps to explain why the bush elephant becomes less active during the heat of the day; with the sun directly overhead it seeks out such shade as may be available–the spreading branches of a flat-topped thorn tree is a particular favourite. More often than not it rests on its feet dozing quietly in the noonday

**Opposite: Asiatic elephants enjoying their daily bath.**

**Left: Mahouts scrub down their charges.**

**Above: African forest elephants in a forest clearing.**

**Overleaf: Elephants take on the colour of the soil with which they dust themselves.**

17

estimated fairly accurately.

Although elephant ivory has been a valuable commodity since long before the dawn of history – even the ancient Britons had a liking for ivory jewellery – there are surprising gaps in our knowledge of it. Many improbable stories have by constant repetition become accepted as authentic, and allegations based on inadequate information have been written into the literature.

The largest tusk still in existence – from an African elephant killed on Kilimanjaro and now in the British Museum of Natural History – weighs 226½ pounds (102·7 kilograms) and is 10 feet 2½ inches (3·1 metres) long; its twin weighs 214 pounds (97 kilograms). The largest tusks of an Asiatic elephant are a pair weighing 161 and 160 pounds (73 and 72·5 kilograms) and measuring 8 feet 9 inches and 8 feet 6½ inches (2·7 metres and 2·6 metres) respectively. But these weights are exceptional. Any tusk that tops the scales at 100 pounds (45·3 kilograms) can be considered an uncommonly fine trophy, and elephants carrying ivory as heavy as this are becoming increasingly rare. Even a century ago, when Selous was hunting north of the Zambezi, he was well satisfied with tusks of 50 pounds (22·7 kilograms) a side.

Elephants with multiple tusks have occasionally been recorded from both Africa and Asia. There are a number of authentic records of four, five, and even seven-tusked elephants, but these are simply abnormal.

Although the tusks of cows are smaller than bulls', rarely, if ever, exceeding 50 pounds (22·7 kilograms), the closer grain of cow ivory makes it more suitable for carving, and thus of a higher quality. Ivory from eastern Africa is whiter and less brittle than West African ivory, and is therefore regarded as superior. In the trade it is known as 'soft' ivory, the West African as 'hard'.

Tusks are, of course, greatly elongated upper incisors. The butt, which is hollow to house the nerve, takes up about one-third of the overall length of the tusk. In a large tusk the circumference of the butt can be anything up to 2 feet (600 millimetres). Broken tusks are an occupational hazard, acquired either in fighting or in lifting heavy objects. Exposure of the nerve causes intense pain; small wonder that a broken-tusked elephant is usually so bad-tempered.

As human beings are either right- or left-handed, so elephants tend to use one tusk more than the other, and an evenly matched pair is a rarity. Minor tusk damage in the form of loss of the tip or chipping of the sides is commonplace; and the tips are, of course, being constantly worn down by normal usage. Adult elephants usually have a groove near the tip of their most-used tusk where the constant action of grass wears a transverse furrow in the ivory.

As ivory is ever-growing, minor damage is gradually made good. The recuperative power of ivory has never been better demonstrated than by a large tusk from Africa which came into the hands of Rowland Ward, the London taxidermists. Embedded in it was a spearhead buried so deeply that it was completely encased in ivory. By a freak chance the spear had presumably struck the tusk in such a way that although the elephant managed to break off the wooden haft, it was unable to dislodge the metal head. Over the years the living ivory gradually grew around it until it was no longer visible.

But the elephant's most remarkable physical feature is unquestionably its trunk.

sun, its only movement being the gentle fanning of its huge ears.

The question of how and when an elephant sleeps has long been in dispute. Gordon Cumming, a well-known sportsman who lived more than a century ago, believed that in areas where they are undisturbed elephants sleep on their sides; this was proved to his satisfaction by the impression of their tusks on the ground. But even as careful an observer of wildlife behaviour as Selous had 'never either seen one actually lying down to rest or found the marks on the ground where one had been lying'. It was generally assumed that elephants invariably slept in a standing position. Only recently have studies of captive animals shown that although by day they certainly do sleep on their feet, they also sometimes sleep in a recumbent position, usually at night.

The elephant's teeth are of unusual interest. Apart from its tusks, which are greatly enlarged upper incisors, the elephant possesses only cheek teeth. Each quadrant of its jaw has only a single cheek tooth, but what is lacking in numbers is made up in size, for each tooth is about 1 foot (300 millimetres) long. These gigantic teeth are used for grinding the vegetation on which the animal lives. The heavy use to which the teeth are put gradually hones them down and, as each tooth becomes worn, it is replaced by another pushing in from behind, up to a maximum of six for each jaw quadrant. The life span of an elephant is as long as its teeth, for after its quota of teeth has been exhausted the animal is no longer able to chew its food, and must therefore die. Knowledge of the average life expectancy of their teeth has enabled the age of elephants to be

Opposite: Dust, applied with the trunk, soothes the elephant's skin.

Whether in Asia (above) or Africa (below) the happiest moment of an elephant's day is when it is immersed in water.

Above: A group of elephants, flanked by attendant egrets, in the Amboseli National Park, Kenya.

Opposite: An old bull leans against a tree while enjoying his midday siesta.

Overleaf: Short of complete immersion, a thorough showering is the next best thing.

Everybody knows that an elephant has a trunk, but how many people have paused to consider what a truly extraordinary organ it is. No other animal has anything quite like it; indeed, possession of a trunk goes a long way to explain why the elephant has been such an outstandingly successful animal.

The trunk is essentially an organ of touch and smell, and as the elephant's sight and hearing are both comparatively poor, its sense of smell is of special importance. Selous went so far as to say that 'there is probably no animal possessed of a keener sense of smell than the elephant'. Fine hairs at the tip of the trunk help to detect scent carried on the breeze.

But the trunk is infinitely more than a sensitive nose; it is a snout which has become so elongated that it functions as a fifth limb. And this is no ordinary limb. As well as being highly mobile, it combines strength with lightness of touch; thus an elephant can as easily pick up a solitary blade of grass as raise a heavy log. Its delicacy is well illustrated by the observation of Lee S. Crandall, of the New York Zoological Park, that he 'once saw a great African bull elephant place the tip of its trunk over a nest of young robins on the fence of his enclosure, test it cautiously, and gently withdraw, leaving the fledglings to be safely reared.' The versatility of the elephant's trunk was also noted by Aristotle when he wrote his famous *Historia Animalium* in the fourth century BC: 'Just, then, as divers are sometimes provided with instruments for respiration, through which they can draw air from above the water, and thus remain for a long time under the sea, so also have elephants been furnished by Nature with their lengthened nostril. . . .'

The main function of the trunk is, of course, to convey food and water to the animal's mouth, but it has many subsidiary uses, made even more effective when used, as it frequently is, in conjunction with the tusks and forefeet. The trunk not only looks rather like a length of reinforced rubber tubing, it is every bit as flexible. This combination of length and mobility enables the animal to reach branches and leaves high above its head, thereby giving the elephant almost the same advantage as the giraffe. It can equally easily pick up objects from the ground, or even from below ground level – particularly useful when drinking. The trunk also allows either of these extremes to be reached with the least possible exertion or change in position of the body, an arrangement which not only has the advantage of conserving energy but, more importantly, permits the elephant to eat and drink without for a moment relaxing its constant watchfulness.

This point can best be seen by comparing the ease with which an elephant drinks with the gymnastics of the giraffe: to get its mouth to water, the giraffe is obliged to go through a protracted sequence of awkward jerks as it thrusts its forelegs farther and farther apart like a novice performing the splits. And having by dint of much effort settled into what appears to be a thoroughly uncomfortable position, the giraffe no sooner takes its first sip of water than it throws up its head in a spasm of nervous anticipation of danger. For the giraffe the act of drinking is clearly something of an ordeal, compared with the elephant's calm and unhurried manner.

While there is some measure of disagreement among professional hunters as to the relative claims of the elephant, rhinoceros, buffalo, lion and leopard – regarded by general consent as the five principal game animals – for the accolade of the 'most dangerous' animal, few would hesitate to award that distinction to the elephant. An enraged elephant, whether cow or bull, bearing down on you out of a cloud of dust, with ears set like a pair of spinnakers, trunk drawn in to its chest, head held high with eyes peering over the tips of its tusks as though lining you up in its sights is, to say the least, unnerving. To add to your discomforture, the elephant often charges to the accompaniment of a blast of high-pitched trumpeting – caused by forcibly expelling air from its trunk – which sounds like an orchestra of outraged demons. Except perhaps for the prospect of imminent hanging, there can be few situations that 'concentrate the mind more wonderfully'.

The almost overwhelming desire to turn and flee has to be balanced against the certain knowledge that if the elephant is determined to press home its attack it can easily outrun you. Only a few months ago, a member of a television crew was trampled to death while filming a charging elephant in Zaïre, only one of many human fatalities at the hands of elephants.

But such incidents, tragic as they are, should not make one think that elephants are monsters of ferociousness. They are, it is true, capable of dealing out death and destruction, for which reason they should be treated with the utmost respect. To attempt to take liberties with them is foolhardy in the extreme. It is equally true that they are placid creatures and, like most wild animals, keener to avoid trouble than to make it. Elephants have learnt from experience to fear no animal but man, the super-predator, and they are understandably nervous in the presence of human beings.

Except for man, an adult elephant has little cause to fear any creature. Even a hungry lion would be unlikely to attack a mature elephant, though it might attempt to take an unguarded calf. Similarly, a pack of hyenas or wild dogs would not hesitate to kill a lone elephant calf if the opportunity occurred. Rennie Bere, former Director of Uganda National Parks, gives an instance of a solitary cow elephant surrounded by a pack of sixteen hyenas: 'She was standing in a very protective position with a young calf between her forelegs. [The warden's] arrival in a Land Rover distracted the attention of the hyenas and allowed the elephant to get away. As she went he saw that the hyenas had attacked already. The calf's hindquarters were lacerated and dripping blood; its tail was hanging by a piece of skin.'

Although incidents of this sort unquestionably happen from time to time, especially in periods of drought when young calves, weakened from exhaustion and lack of food, become more easily separated from the group, the female elephant is generally a devoted mother; she is also generally assured of help from a bevy of attentive cows constantly alert for trouble who at the first hint of danger rally to her support. No canine pack, however large or famished, would dare attack the protective phalanx of mature elephants encircling their young – the normal formation adopted by elephants in the face of serious threat.

The principal difference between the ecology of the two living species is that the African bush elephant – though not the smaller forest form – is essentially an animal

of the savannas, the open grasslands dotted with greater or lesser density of tree cover which extend over much of the medium rainfall areas of Africa, whereas the Asiatic elephant is a forest dweller. This helps to account for the relative difference in the size of the two species' ears: by living in the forest the Asiatic elephant has largely resolved the problem of overheating, whereas the African elephant, living as it does in open country and thus much more exposed to the sun, is in greater need of some means of regulating its body temperature.

Although elephants tend naturally to concentrate in areas where conditions are most to their liking, they also show remarkable adaptability to a wide variety of other types of habitat, which helps to explain the elephant's success in clinging to existence against increasingly heavy odds.

It is probably no exaggeration to suggest that in its feeding habits the elephant is more adaptable than any other large land animal. The contrast between the narrowly specialized food requirements of most herbivorous animals and the broad feeding habits of the elephant is very pronounced. Although the Asiatic elephant is primarily a browser and the African elephant a grazer – in parts of Uganda the elephant's diet is said to comprise 88 per cent grass – both species modify their feeding habits when their preferred food is scarce, the African elephant stepping up its consumption of leaves, twigs and shoots and the Asiatic eating more grass. The African elephant will, moreover, consume many types of plants – in Tsavo National Park, more than 100 different kinds have been estimated, including some that are too coarse for most grazing animals. When

The different habitats in which elephants can live cover a broad spectrum, from dense tropical rain forest to near-desert, and from coastal lowlands to mountain forests, even extending above the upper limits of tree growth towards the snow-line as, for example, on the massifs of Mount Kenya, Kilimanjaro and the Ruwenzori Range. Tracks of elephant have been found up to a height of 15,000 feet (4,570 metres) on Kilimanjaro.

Elephants do not, of course, live permanently on either the bleak alpine moorlands or in intensely arid regions – these they visit only occasionally, either as dry season grazing areas or when trekking from one feeding ground to another – but the fact that they are able to make use of marginal areas greatly expands their range, thus giving them an advantage over less adaptable species.

other food is scarce, elephants sometimes supplement their diet with bark and the fibrous wood of certain trees, either by lightly chewing small branches and rolling them around the tongue to peel off the bark or by using their tusks and trunks to strip it from the trees. Elephants will also dig in the ground for the roots and tubers of drought-resistant plants and shrubs: some semi-desert plants, such as *Adenia globosa*, have enormous underground bulbs, resembling large boulders, which contain substantial quantities of water. Selous saw 'acres of sandy ground dug into holes by a large herd of elephants, but the digging was done with their forefeet and not with their tusks. When by this means a root was laid bare, the elephant would prise it up with its tusks and, after breaking it in two, pull the tapering end out with his trunk.'

**Opposite, top:** An Asiatic elephant on its way to work carries a bunch of palm fronds in its trunk.

**Opposite, below:** An African elephant feeding in tall vegetation.

**Above:** The manner in which the trunk is used for feeding is shown in this photograph of an African elephant.

The normal diet of grasses and foliage is also supplemented by seasonal wild fruits to which elephants are very partial; elephants are in fact so fond of fruit – to say nothing of berries, wild celery, wild ginger, bamboo shoots and seed pods of many kinds – that they are prepared to trek long distances to find it. A particular favourite is the fruit of the doum palm. Where these palm trees grow abundantly – as, for instance, along the banks of the Uaso Nyiro River in northern Kenya – windfalls litter the ground in season, much of the fruit in the early stages of fermentation. The elephants find this ripe fruit almost irresistible, and the effect of their overindulgence is much the same as a human being having too much alcohol. Tipsy elephants, somewhat unsteady on their feet, are not in this case a fantasy of Walt Disney's fertile imagination.

To dislodge growing fruit or berries, elephants often resort to vigorously shaking the branches or even to uprooting entire trees for, as Sir Samuel Baker, pioneer explorer of the Nile headwaters, tells us, 'no food is so much coveted by elephants'. He mentions in particular the African elephant's liking for the 'desert date' (*Balanites aegyptiaca*), known by the Arabs as *heglik*, and he describes an occasion in the Sudan when an elephant 'of extraordinary size moved slowly towards us, until he halted beneath a tall, spreading *heglik*. This tree must have been nearly 3 feet in diameter, and was about 30 feet high from the ground to the first branch; it was therefore impossible for the elephant to gather the coveted fruit. To root up such a tree would have been out of the question. The elephant paused for a short time, as though considering; he then butted his forehead suddenly against the trunk. I could not have believed the effect: this large tree, which was equal in appearance to the average size of park-timber, quivered in every branch to such a degree, that had a person taken refuge from an elephant, and thought himself secure in the top, he would have found it difficult to hold on.'

When food is plentiful and the herd undisturbed, the elephant is a casual feeder. It will sometimes nonchalantly extract tufts of grass by kicking them gently with the horny nails of its forefeet to sever the stems, simultaneously pulling with its trunk; it then bashes the grass against its front legs to knock off any soil before thrusting it into its mouth. But during the dry season when food is scarce and the elephant is faced with the problem of obtaining the 3 hundredweight (152 kilograms) of food which form an adult's

28

**The Asiatic elephant (opposite) is essentially a forest-dweller, whereas the African bush elephant (left) is primarily a species of the open grassland savannas.**

normal daily intake, life becomes a desperate struggle for survival. The elephant roams widely across country, gleaning dried sticks and withered vegetation which would normally be rejected, sometimes pushing over trees to feed on the upper branches lying beyond its reach, and often leaving a trail of destruction in its wake.

Mobility is a characteristic of the elephant herd, and it is during the dry season – in Africa a regular feature of the annual climatic cycle – that mobility becomes of such vital importance to survival. During the rainy season the African grasslands are covered with innumerable waterholes, filling hollows and natural depressions and re-plenished by every passing shower. Both fodder and abundant water are close at hand, and the needs of the herds are met with little effort. While the rains are on, therefore, the herds have neither cause nor inclination to wander, and during this season of plenty they remain in small, widely scattered, sedentary groups.

This leisurely existence changes radically once the rains have ended. As the dry season advances, the natural waterholes gradually dry out and the scattered herds are forced to fall back on what little permanent water they can find. By the time the dry season reaches its searing climax, permanent water is generally available only in the larger rivers, and these, of course, are few and far between.

At the height of the dry season, therefore, almost all the species that require to drink regularly are concentrated in the vicinity – or at least within trekking distance – of the permanent rivers. These heavy concentrations ot grazing and browsing animals soon consume the vegetation in the area until eventually almost nothing remains. The herds are then faced with a dilemma; on the one hand they are tied to the river for water, while on the other they must move farther and farther away from it for food.

It is at this time that the elephants' superior powers of mobility and endurance prove such an advantage: they range deep into the hinterland – frequently covering up to 50 miles (80 kilometres) in a night – so that

**Above: A boulder comes in handy as a rubbing post.**

**Top right: Although primarily a grass-eater, the African elephant also browses on foliage.**

**Right: A family of African elephants on trek.**

they are well beyond the reach of most other animals competing with them for food. As the need to water regularly is as compelling as the need for food, the herds spend the latter part of the dry season almost constantly on trek between the river and their grazing grounds.

Under exceptionally severe conditions, however, this pattern can change. Daphne Sheldrick, wife of the Tsavo National Park Warden, records that at the height of the great Tsavo drought of 1970–71, the elephants 'made no attempt to move where conditions were less critical . . . [but] died where they were in large numbers, . . . [In places] had they moved only 5 miles either up or down stream they would have found a plentiful supply of food.'

Apart from the few large rivers, the only other sources of permanent water available at the height of the dry season in many of the more arid parts of Africa lie underground, beneath the surface of sand rivers. Sand rivers accumulate water during the rainy season, but only rarely do they flow in the conventional sense. Storm water, often falling at a distance, may cause them suddenly to erupt into flood and, for a few hours or at most a few days, the normally dry river roars down in spate, sweeping aside everything in its path. But such affluence is only briefly bestowed and as quickly withdrawn. Within a short while the flash flood has spent itself, leaving no more than a trail of broken branches and other debris to mark its course. For the remainder of the year there is no visible flow. But the absence of surface water is deceptive, for the sandy bed acts as a gigantic sponge, absorbing enormous quantities of water and retaining it below the ground almost indefinitely.

Where permanent rivers are lacking, the sand rivers act as natural reservoirs, their presence indicated by narrow strips of trees and other riverbank vegetation whose roots enable them to exploit the subterranean moisture. Often these sand rivers hold the only permanent water over a wide area; the problem is to tap them.

It is then that the elephant undertakes a function which almost no other animal can perform; by digging with its tusks and forefeet and using its trunk to suck out the sand, the elephant sinks holes through the dry river bed into the underlying water. At the height of the dry season these holes may have to be 3 or 4 feet (0·9 or 1·2 metres) deep. Water then slowly percolates into the hole until it resembles a miniature well.

Swaying gently on its forefeet, the

elephant uses its trunk partly to scoop and partly to suck sand from the hole before squirting it to one side. Infinite patience is necessary, for it takes some time for the water to seep into the hole. Between every trunkful the elephant must pause while the hole slowly refills: if he is too eager, he will find the solution contains more sand than water.

The process may take a long time—too long usually for the other animals waiting impatiently for the elephant to finish its work and make way for them. But as they are incapable of digging the holes themselves, they have no alternative but to bide their time until the elephant has done. When at last, nonchalantly spraying a final trunkful of water across its shoulders, the elephant eventually ambles away, the animals which have been waiting in the background close

will have dug a great many holes—usually sufficient to accommodate most of the more fastidious animals which have come to drink.

An enterprising baboon attempting to clear a blocked hole with its hands soon becomes discouraged and moves off to try its luck elsewhere. A shy gazelle, anxiously awaiting its opportunity, moves timidly towards a vacant hole, thrusting its delicate muzzle only briefly into the opening before withdrawing to glance nervously around for sight or sound of predators lurking in the nearby shadows. For the predators take full advantage of these nocturnal gatherings to ambush their prey.

By the time the first shafts of dawn herald the start of a new day, the overnight drinking session has come to an end. The various species of animals which have spent the hours of darkness quenching their thirst, have all

**Above: Tusks and trunk are used for digging either for water or salt. Here an elephant is extracting salt from a 'lick'.**

**Opposite: Regular watering is an indispensable feature of the elephant's life. A group of African elephants at a waterhole.**

in to slake their thirst. A rhinoceros, by virtue of its size, is usually first on the scene, snuffing and snorting with undisguised frustration as it tries to thrust its snout into a hole which, although adequate for the slender trunk of an elephant, was not designed to accommodate a rhinoceros's outsize head and horns. The rhino's clumsy scrabbling frequently damages the hole so severely that its sides cave in, making it useless for other animals. But a herd of elephants

dispersed. As the sun mounts higher in the heavens, dissolving the last lingering shadows, hordes of brilliantly coloured butterflies alight to suck the final traces of moisture from the still-damp sand. Before long they too disperse among the trees on either bank, and innumerable hoofprints in the sand are all that remains to attest the night's activities, and to proclaim to anyone able to interpret the signs the crucial role of the elephant as Nature's water-diviner.

# FAMILY LIFE

Only within the last few years, and as the result of the patient work of a few dedicated naturalists, has the social organization of the elephant begun to be understood. Although it was recognized that elephants are gregarious animals, sometimes assembling in massive concentrations, little was known about the make-up of the herd and its social structure. Small groups of females and calves were as likely to be encountered as clusters of bulls or herds of mixed sex. The make-up of the herds seemed so inconsistent that it appeared to defy rational explanation. It was clear that an understanding of the basic herd structure could not be achieved by casual or fragmentary observations.

It was not until Iain Douglas-Hamilton undertook his patient study in the 1960s, the results of which are published in his book *Among the Elephants*, that a clear pattern began to emerge. His brilliant pioneer work, spread over more than four years in Tanzania's Lake Manyara National Park, cast a refreshingly clear light on a subject which until then had remained obscure. He discovered that the social organization of the elephant was founded upon the family unit, made up of closely related cows and their calves under the leadership of a mature female, the matriarch. Larger gatherings are of only a temporary nature, often remaining together for no more than a few hours before once again dispersing into smaller groups. However many units gather together and however much they intermingle, the family remains the basic unit to which each individual elephant owes its primary loyalty and to which its ties are absolute.

Iain Douglas-Hamilton's study also

Left: The family unit, under the leadership of a matriarch, forms the basis of the elephant's social organization.

Above: The breeding of domesticated elephants is generally, but not invariably, discouraged. This calf, in Thailand, was probably born soon after its mother was captured.

showed that several family units – them- selves almost certainly united by blood ties – live in loose association, coming together frequently and seldom wandering more than a few hundred yards from each other. These multi-family associations he terms 'kinship groups'. He concluded that a similar family unit social organization applied to all the other cow–calf groups in the Park, of which there were at least forty-eight. The average size of the family units was ten elephants, and most of these belonged as well to larger kinship groups. Family units who were members of the kinship group might split up for a few days and go to opposite ends of the Park, but they would always join later and continue to keep company.'

Iain Douglas-Hamilton's observations on social structure and behaviour are, of course, applicable only to Manyara where he carried out his study. Until comparable studies are done in other areas, it will be im- possible to say that the Manyara pattern is of wider application though, in the absence of contrary evidence, it seems reasonable to

assume that it will be.

The size of these family units is of course variable; but, generally speaking, each numbers about a dozen individual animals, ranging in age from the matriarch herself to newborn calves. The intermingling of family units sometimes leads to the establish- ment of herds, which can be very large. One of the most spectacular is at Kichwamba, in Uganda, where from the edge of the escarp- ment overlooking the western branch of the Great Rift Valley it is sometimes possible to see more than 1,000 elephants foraging among the lush grasslands far below. The spectacle is made even more memorable by the distant backdrop of the Ruwenzori Range, the fabled Mountains of the Moon. But these huge gatherings are brief, indi- vidual units soon breaking away to resume their separate existence.

When a family unit becomes too large and cumbersome, part of it may separate from the parent body and establish itself independent- ly. Conversely, if a family unit loses its leader the surviving remnant may attach itself to

another unit into which it will gradually become absorbed.

A feeling of affection between individual members of a family unit is a very marked feature of the elephant's social life. This characteristic gentleness and tenderness may seem strangely incongruous in so huge and powerful an animal, but it is a feature which has unquestionably played an im- portant part in the success of the elephant as a species.

The individual derives its strength from the group, and the group from the collective action of the individuals comprising it. Social behaviour is the means by which the group controls and disciplines each indi- vidual and subordinates the needs of the individual to those of the group as a whole.

There are occasions when discipline may even override parental affection, particu- larly where food and water are concerned. An adult cow will not hesitate to thrust a calf, even its own, out of the way when food or water are in short supply. Naturally, this behaviour varies greatly according to the

temperament of the individual animals.

The strength, stability and cohesion of the group is a natural consequence of the family structure. Leadership of the group, unquestioned and unchallenged, automatically devolves upon its senior member, a mature female whose authority every member of the group respects without demur. Normally each family unit consists of the leader's own offspring and their progeny, and thus every member of the group is usually descended from the leader herself.

In this way a hierarchy, acceptable to all, evolves spontaneously within each family unit. The harmonious relationships between the individual members of the unit rule out any likelihood of a struggle for supremacy. The matriarch embodies the qualities of leadership by virtue of her age and experience; the younger members of the unit accept her authority without question through having been brought up to hold her in esteem and look to her for guidance and direction.

The death of the matriarch is not followed by the clash of rivals bidding for dominance; the transition is swift and smooth, automatic and unopposed, her place being at once filled by the next most senior and experienced member of the unit.

Within the unit there are, naturally, family squabbles, but these lapses in behaviour are invariably settled more or less amicably, for each of the individuals concerned knows her own standing in the hierarchy and respects the status of her seniors. When an inferior elephant greets a superior member of the hierarchy, it may denote its submission by extending its trunk and thrusting the tip into the superior's mouth. Where young and experienced animals are concerned, any tendency towards disruptiveness is met by disciplinary action firmly administered by an older member of the unit.

On occasions when there is temporary intermingling of different family units, as for instance at waterholes, problems inevitably arise, particularly when water is scarce, but these difficulties are usually resolved peaceably. Differences between individuals are

**Above: Elephants are highly companionable animals. Part of a family unit watering in the Murchison Falls National Park, Uganda.**

**Left: The strength and security of the individual elephant are greatly enhanced by being a member of a herd. A family unit at Amboseli, Kenya.**

settled by means of the 'threat display' which has the advantage of allowing decisions to be taken without resort to force.

This was first brought home to me when spending a night beside the Tiva, a sand river in the Tsavo National Park, the full moon lighting the scene so brilliantly that the movement of every animal could be seen almost as clearly as by day. The foreground was dominated by a scattering of solitary elephants patiently digging for water in the sandy riverbed. They had been occupied in this way for some time when a latecomer appearing out of the shadows strode purposefully towards an elephant which, having finished digging, was patiently waiting for water to seep into the hole. The two appeared evenly matched, and as the newcomer seemed intent on taking possession of the hole, a fight looked like a foregone conclusion. But

nothing of the kind occurred. The owner of the hole stood her ground; turning slightly to face the newcomer, she merely swung open her ears until they stood out at right angles to her body like a suit of sails. This seemingly trivial action was sufficient to stop the newcomer in her tracks; barely pausing, she backed a few paces before turning and moving away.

Reaction to real or imaginary danger naturally differs according to temperament. Some elephants remain calm and placid; others react violently by charging without hesitation. Anger or fear are expressed in a variety of ways, from shaking or tossing the head, through body swaying, trunk twirling and foot shuffling to kicking up dust with the feet or spraying it over the head with the trunk. Or it may take the form of wrenching tufts of grass from the ground and hurling

them either into the air or towards the object of dislike. Iain Douglas-Hamilton describes these actions as 'typical displacement activities', adding that 'in elephants they were a great help to me in predicting their behaviour. The more marked these activities the less likely the elephant was to charge. Very often the most impressive threat displays emanated from the most frightened elephants which were unlikely to make a serious attack.'

If these relatively mild but nonetheless meaningful gestures fail to achieve their purpose, the animal's fear may manifest itself in hostility and the threat display turn into the threat charge. But few threat charges are carried through. Generally, of course, they don't have to be, for usually the elephant's antagonist does not wait to learn whether or not the charge is in earnest. The elephant

Left: Touch plays an important part in the social life of the elephant. Here two elephants touch each other with their trunks in greeting (below).

Below: The threat display. An elephant reacting to possible danger by tossing its head, spreading its ears, and twirling its trunk.

Overleaf: The preliminary stages of the threat display. The spreading ears and raised head indicate that this tusker is alert to possible danger.

therefore achieves its purpose without the need to press its charge home. But, when overcome by fear, even a normally placid elephant can be dangerous, and to be treated with respect.

The most impressive threat display which I can personally vouch for happened when I was accompanying David Sheldrick, Warden of the Tsavo National Park. We were driving at little more than walking pace along a narrow game track when a cow elephant with calf at foot came unexpectedly at us from one side. As she closed with us, David slowly increased speed, obliging her to alter course to conform. In her blind fury she collided at full tilt with a dead tree lying immediately in her path with such force that the tree appeared simply to disintegrate. Out of the corner of my eye I had an unforgettable glimpse of a veritable shower of foliage and shattered branches cascading, seemingly in slow motion, to the ground.

At the time I was convinced that this was a determined charge but, with the benefit of hindsight, it seems more likely to have been an example of the phenomenon termed by Niko Tinbergen, an authority on animal behaviour, as 'redirected aggression'. In other words, the elephant was reacting to danger not by attacking the animal or object causing that fear but by taking it out on another object – in much the same way that human beings give vent to their pent-up emotion by hurling crockery.

Occasionally, of course, the charge is pressed home, and when that happens the result can be devastating. Iain Douglas-Hamilton relates how his car was attacked and almost destroyed by a particularly aggressive group of elephants '. . . a huge bow-tusked female . . . without uttering a sound, nor pausing in her stride, plunged her tusks up to the gums into the body of my Land-Rover. . . . The first shock threw the car half round. The elephant pulled out her tusks and thrust them in again. . . . Now more elephants with babies in the forefront burst out of the bush on the right and joined in the attack. . . . It felt half-way between being a rugger ball in a scrum, and a dinghy overtaken by three contradictory tidal waves. The car teetered on the point of balance but just missed overturning. Tusks were thrust in and withdrawn with great vigour. Loud and continuous trumpeting rent the air, together with that fatal sound of tearing metal. . . . A huge late-comer with as much zeal as the rest put together now came into contact with the front. One wing folded up like paper and a tusk went through the radiator. She stabbed again and wrenched her embedded tusks upwards like a demented fork lift. Then digging her tusks in again she charged, and the Land-Rover was carried backwards at high speed for 35 yards until it squashed up against an ant heap surmounted by a small tree. . . .'

Although they are obviously capable of being extremely aggressive, elephants are at the same time very solicitous of other members of their family unit, particularly of calves. When danger threatens, the adults close up and form a defensive circle, facing outwards and screening the calves with their bodies. But their solicitude sometimes goes much further than simply defending others. Reports that elephants sometimes go to the help of injured companions were for a long time dismissed as mere travellers' tales, but there is now positive evidence that such stories are no exaggeration.

Below: Elephants can if necessary cover a surprising distance in a day. By using the extended walk, shown here, they can move considerably faster than a man, and they can keep it up for many hours on end.

Opposite: Sometimes elephants congregate in immense herds. This aerial photograph shows part of a huge herd in the Murchison Falls National Park, Uganda.

Bruce Kinloch, former Chief Game Warden of Uganda, for example, tells how a bull elephant which he had wounded during elephant control operations was aided by four cows, two of them 'leaning inwards to support him with their powerful shoulders.... Behind him, their massive foreheads against his rump, were two more cows. The whole group was moving slowly but steadily through the water, throwing up a small bow-wave that fanned out through the swamp in a broad arrow of muddy ripples, on which the reeds swayed and tossed like wind-blown corn.'

Toni Harthoorn had a similar experience when tranquillizing elephants: 'One female which went down was attended by the entire herd, which beat a solid path round her, half lifting her on their tusks till she was able to stand.'

Even more remarkable is Daphne Sheldrick's account of a bull 'in no way connected with the herd, placing his tusks beneath the stomach of a small calf that had left its unit to venture deeper than usual into a water-hole.... until it was safely reunited with its mother, the bull, with gentle concern, stood by, prepared to support it should it get into difficulties.'

We now know that elephants have a particular area, or territory, which varies in size from one family unit to another and frequently overlaps that of neighbouring units. A territory is not exclusive to any one unit nor – as with so many animal species – is it defended against intrusion by others. In fact, the opposite appears to be more common: far from repelling other groups, elephants seem to prefer the presence of others of their kind.

Each family unit is thoroughly familiar with its own territory, around which it slowly travels from one spot to another. Elephants are continually on the move, governed by the seasonal availability of water and different types of food, by shade, and by disturbance. A family unit may, for instance, have to travel some distance each day from its feeding area to its drinking place, or spend the early morning and evening in open country and the hottest time of the day in forest or thicket. Nor, of course, will a family unit use every part of its territory: much of it may seldom, if ever, be visited.

The size of elephant territories varies enormously according to the prevailing ecological conditions. At Manyara, where conditions are unusually favourable, territories are relatively small; but in more arid areas – as, for instance, in and around Tsavo National Park – where a much more extensive area is necessary to meet the animals' requirements, territories are correspondingly larger.

Before close human settlement and intensive development restricted the movement of the herds, elephant territories may have been larger than they are today. The true extent of the larger elephant territories remains a matter of conjecture, but the records of the early naturalists and explorers in Africa give an indication of how extensive these seasonal movements sometimes were. In Kenya, for example, there was a regular exodus of elephants from the arid Northern Frontier Province to the Lorian Swamp, the Tana and Galana rivers, and to the forested highlands of Mount Kenya, the Aberdares, and the Matthews and Ndoto ranges. The herds remained in these dry-season grazing areas until the beginning of the long rains, when they retraced their steps to their wet-

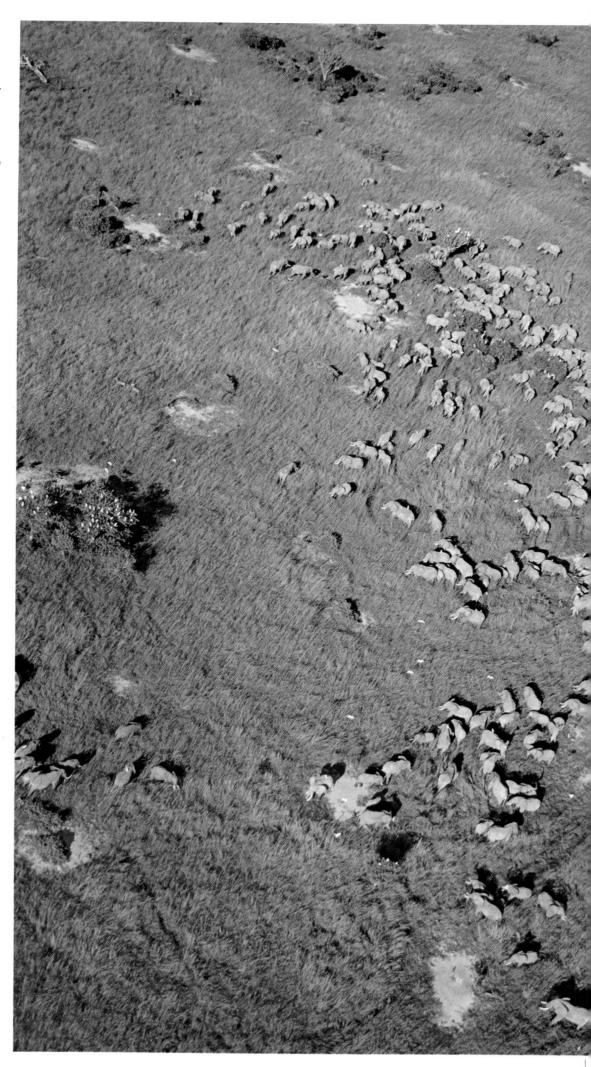

season grazing areas in the lowlands.

Another regular migration took place in northern Uganda. At certain seasons elephants were abundant in Karamoja, but when conditions became unfavourable some moved into the Sudan, others into Acholi. They would spend part of the year in the hills and mountain ranges in the northern part of the region before moving down onto the plains, apparently attracted by the ripening fruit of the borassus palms lining the sand rivers.

These seasonal migrations are sparked off by the need to obtain food and water, often to feed on a favourite fruit or berry or for the seasonal bounty of fallen acacia pods – an unfailing source of food for many herbivorous animals. The elephants probably follow a regular pattern, the herds always using the same routes between the dry-season and wet-season grazing areas. The passage of generations of elephants has carved well-beaten trails, worn smooth by the tread of innumerable padded feet winding up escarpments and over mountain ranges, skirting chasms and precipices and invariably following the gentlest gradients. The early European settlers found the Kenya Highlands crisscrossed by elephant trails which, to judge from appearances, had been in regular use for many years. As Blayney Percival, Kenya's first Game 'Ranger', remarked, 'the elephant is the best judge of gradients in the world'. The road-engineering capabilities of the elephant were also noted by Denis Lyell, who commented on 'their wonderfully chosen footpaths over high ranges. These paths, often used for ages, are very smooth and, in level country, one could almost use a bicycle along them. . . . A re-

**For the first year of its life an elephant calf is seldom far from its mother (right) or following close at heel (opposite).**

44

markable point about elephants is the way they surmount hilly ground, choosing always the easiest gradient; so human beings crossing such country cannot do better than follow them. . . .'

When on the move elephants can cover the ground surprisingly quickly. Their seemingly slow gait is deceptive for their stride is long, enabling them to maintain a steady speed of 5 or 6 miles (8 or 9·6 kilometres) an hour for many hours on end. If pressed, they can move even faster. In this way, moving mainly by night and resting only briefly during the heat of the day, they are able to travel remarkably long distances. They eat as they go, using their trunks to pluck vegetation without pausing in their stride. Normally, of course, elephants are active mainly by day, but under abnormal conditions, such as drought or in places where they are constantly harried by man, they may change their habits and become nocturnal.

Equally surprising is the manner in which such an enormous animal can fade into its background. This struck me forcibly when I was flying a light aircraft over Kenya's Aberdare Range. Almost beneath my feet I spotted a large herd moving up a broad forest track leading to the moorlands. Quickly circling to take a closer look, I completed my circuit only to find that the entire herd had disappeared as effectively as if it had been a figment of my imagination.

Whether on the move or placidly feeding in familiar surroundings, elephants are normally accompanied by a gentle rumbling sound, rather like contented purring, which forms a constant background noise to their activities. Few aspects of elephant behaviour have been more puzzling, particularly because these noises seem to be switched on and off at will. Most accounts state that the rumbling comes from the stomach, but these so-called 'tummy rumbles' are in fact made in the throat in the form of a gargling sound; on occasion this throaty gurgle is transferred to the back of the trunk when, magnified and diffused in the long nasal passages, it emerges as a more resonant sound. Only recently has it been realised that elephant rumblings are contact calls by means of which individual animals keep in touch. Continual rumbling is a sure indication of well-being; if it suddenly stops the other members of the herd know they need to be on the alert.

According to Crandall, the Asiatic elephant's warning or alarm signal is a 'hollow, resonant sound (made) by tapping "back-handed" on a hard surface with its trunk,

the tip of which has been turned upward'.

In most animal species, the maternal instincts are focused either primarily or exclusively on the most recently born young. So strong is this instinct that the parents normally firmly eject the young of the previous litter from the family circle in preparation for the impending birth. The newborn thus receive undivided parental attention free from the competition, sometimes the downright hostility, of other larger siblings.

With elephants, however, the situation is altogether different: there is nothing in the least unusual in seeing three, occasionally even four, calves ranging in age from newborn to teenager living harmoniously with their mother. As elephants are not weaned until an advanced age (sometimes as much as eight or nine years), it is perfectly normal for a cow elephant to continue suckling an older calf at the same time as her younger—often simultaneously, one from each nipple.

The calves do not necessarily suckle exclusively from their own mother; they do not hesitate to tap any other female willing to accommodate them. Sometimes a cow will adopt an orphaned calf and raise it as her own. The question of jealousy does not seem to arise. Indeed, far from resenting the appearance of a new calf, the older calves seem positively to welcome it, actively helping their mother to look after it, guarding it, playing with it, teaching it. A particularly close relationship may develop between an older and a younger calf born of the same parent: the older calf assists its mother in looking after its younger brother or sister, in the process forging a bond that remains unbroken for life.

Usually the other members of the family

unit are extremely well disposed towards newborn calves, fondling them with their trunks, helping them to their feet, responding at once to their shrill cries for help, and being generally protective. Referring to the Asiatic elephant, Fred Kurt, who participated in the Smithsonian Institution's Ceylon Elephant Survey, makes the point that the rearing of a wild elephant calf is such an exacting and time-consuming occupation that the attention of 'more than one adult is required. To look after a baby is an exhausting 24-hour task. As an adult elephant normally feeds during 18 hours in 24, it is essential that the job of looking after the babies is shared amongst various members of the herd . . . who not only take upon themselves the task of protecting and looking after the baby, but also assist in its feeding by preparing grass and breaking branches . . . . Babies are usually grouped together in what might be termed a nursery. The nursery is in charge of one adult animal, which is relieved from time to time by others.'

The elephant's need for physical contact is very strong and it uses its trunk to satisfy this tactile need. It is particularly pronounced in the mother–calf relationship, where physical contact of one kind or another is almost constant–and reassuring to both. Thus, apart from its purely practical functions, the elephant's trunk is an instrument of enormous social and psychological importance, comparable with social grooming among monkeys and other primates.

The affection and devotion shown by elephants is vividly illustrated by Daphne Sheldrick's account of a very young orphaned bull calf which suddenly became ill when she was attempting to raise it. A larger female calf actively assisted the Sheldricks in lifting up the sick calf by placing her tusks and trunk underneath its limp body and propping it on its feet while they fed it with milk and, later, with oranges and sweet potato tops: 'We thought the appearance of the oranges would be the moment when Eleanor's liking for them would outweigh her concern for her sick foster-child, for normally, whenever any oranges are produced, she barges and shoves everyone aside in her eagerness to get at them and stuff as many as possible into her mouth in the shortest time. It was surprising, therefore, that on this occasion, she stood by quietly and watched them being cut and fed to Bukaneza, demonstrating amazing self-sacrifice, and intelligence, for it was as though she recognized that Bukaneza's need was the greater on this occasion.'

A striking example of the mother–calf bond was a report from the Uganda National Parks of a cow elephant which carried her dead calf for several days, holding the corpse between her jaw and her shoulder, and placing it on the ground only when she stopped to feed or drink.

There are, of course, exceptions to this affectionate and tolerant attitude. Some mothers, particularly those giving birth for the first time, tend to be nervous about their calves, over-reacting to real or imaginary difficulties and dangers and generally behaving in a thoroughly neurotic manner. The more mature females, experienced in the problems of calf-rearing, are normally of a more placid disposition.

Calves remain within the bosom of the family unit until adolescence. With female calves this close family relationship continues long after maturity is reached, the

**Below: From the earliest age elephants take readily to water. Here an Asiatic elephant calf enjoys its daily dip.**

**Opposite: When no open water is available a swamp will do just as well. A cow elephant and her calf in reedbeds at Amboseli National Park, Kenya.**

Right: An African forest elephant in open country.

Below: Unlike most animals, the cow elephant's teats are situated between her forelegs.

Opposite: The young calf suckles with its mouth, not its trunk.

bonds of affection forged in earliest calfhood continuing for the rest of their life. There are few other animals, apart from man, to which this remark could apply.

Within such a matriarchal society maternal instincts are exceptionally powerful. Even before she reaches puberty the female calf displays latent maternal instincts in her attitude towards her younger brothers and sisters, in the course of which she acquires knowledge and experience that later prove invaluable when the time comes to raise calves of her own.

Only rarely has anyone actually been present at the birth of a wild elephant. The expectant cow moves a short distance away from the group, generally accompanied by one or more female attendants, though whether the latter assist at the birth or merely guard the mother is uncertain. While the

mother stands exhausted by her ordeal, the newborn calf – weighing about 250 pounds (133 kilograms) and a little under 3 feet (915 millimetres) at the shoulder – is assisted by the trunks of the attentive 'midwives' to stand, swaying unsteadily, under her belly. Although at first very shaky on its legs, the calf, encouraged by its mother's gentle nuzzling, is able within a surprisingly short space of time to stand erect and to find her teats which, unlike those of most animals, are situated between her forelegs. Until it learns to be certain of the location of the teats, the calf explores with hopeful expectancy every part of its mother's anatomy within reach, as well as the underparts of any other cow or older calf which happens to be near. It uses its mouth to suckle, curling its tiny trunk to one side or above its head to get it out of the way. Calves take some time

to learn to use their trunks. For the first year or so they drink with their mouths, and are at rather a loss to know quite what to do with their trunks. Only gradually, by a process of trial and error, do they acquire the knack.

Within two days of birth the baby elephant is sufficiently strong on its feet to keep up with the movements of the family unit. For the first year or so of its life the young calf remains close to its mother, seldom leaving her side. As the calf gets older, the concern shown by the cow for her offspring gradually becomes less intensive. The calf wanders farther from its mother, becoming increasingly independent and joining in the rough-and-tumble of the older calves.

The long gestation period of about 22 months and the gap of at least one year, possibly two, between giving birth and being able to conceive again means that even under

favourable circumstances a female elephant cannot be expected to reproduce more often than about once every fourth year. Yet, despite the wide gap between births, she is extremely productive: the effective reproductive life of a cow elephant is about 35 years, and her potential is thus about eight or nine calves. And as she is a very conscientious mother, a high proportion of these calves can be expected to reach maturity.

To counterbalance this productiveness, elephants, like other species, are subject to some natural mechanism for the regulation of their numbers. This is achieved by such means as delaying sexual maturity, disrupting the breeding cycle, greater intervals between calving, and heavier calf mortality. In Uganda, for example, the confinement of elephants within the Murchison Falls National Park resulted in a threefold in-

crease in the interval between birth and conception. Richard Laws, in his work on elephants in Uganda, believes that these natural controls are triggered by rainfall: good seasonal rains mean an abundance of plant food which stimulates reproduction, whereas poor rains mean less food and consequent lowering of the conception rate. In a poor season the harsh living conditions will also result in a higher than normal death rate, thereby reducing overall numbers.

Quite early in life, the calf sprouts a pair of milk tusks, which are shed when the permanent tusks emerge behind them. This generally happens during the second or third year, but it varies widely from one individual to another. By the time the permanent tusks appear, the calf has already begun to indulge in communal play. In the sparring matches

**The happiest time of an elephant's life is when it is in contact with water. All cares and anxieties seem to be cast aside as it relaxes and plays in the water.**

that are a regular feature of growing up, the young calves wrestle by twining their trunks around each other, the clash of tusk against tiny tusk causing them to trumpet with mock fury or assumed indignation. But such play seldom degenerates into violence: where, as often happens, the two contestants are unevenly matched, the older calf will use only sufficient strength to restrain the younger.

There is much more to this high-spirited play than mere exuberance: communal play provides calves with opportunities for strengthening links with others of their kind, and for learning discipline and control, self-reliance and tolerance as preparation for adult life.

Elephants seem to be aware of the power they carry in their tusks. Perhaps the rough-and-tumble of calf play teaches them to avoid using their tusks in an offensive manner –

though sometimes an adult may be provoked into administering discipline so drastically that a calf's ears may be torn and its skin pierced until the blood flows. Normally, though, it is only when elephants really mean business – as, for instance, when rival bulls clash – that the tusks used aggressively. The result can then be overwhelming. Rangers in the Tsavo National Park discovered the remains of a gigantic bull elephant with a wound showing that it had died from a rival's tusk piercing its skull like a harpoon.

Although female elephants normally remain all their lives attached to the family unit into which they are born, the males behave differently. As puberty approaches, the young bulls become increasingly obstreperous, indulging not only in mock fighting but in experimental mounting. In this they are not over-particular whether

they mount the younger females or one another. If a young female tries to stand up to an amorous young bull she will almost certainly be chased or constantly pestered; only if she has the backing of a mature female can she hope to see him off.

Eventually, when about twelve years of age, the behaviour of the adolescent male becomes so intolerable that he has to be banished from the family unit. His attempts to rejoin the strictly matriarchal society with which he has been associated since birth are firmly resisted by the mature females. Torn between reluctance to abandon the security of family life and the realization that his presence will no longer be tolerated, he wanders alone on the periphery of the group, out of sight but within rumbling distance. In this way he follows the movements of his family, occasionally having brief contact

with individual females who have temporarily strayed farther than usual from the matriarch; but never again will he be allowed to have a permanent place in any family circle. In such a matriarchal society the presence of mature bulls is tolerated only when a cow comes on heat. At that time the two animals concerned show every sign of affection, caressing each other with their trunks and placing the tips of their trunks in each other's mouths.

Eventually the young bulls form separate bachelor herds but, divested of the family bond, these rootless associations have no permanence. Young bulls meeting with others of their kind will often indulge in desultory sparring, which sometimes develops into serious fighting. By testing the strength of their rivals a loose hierarchy is established. An individual's acceptance of

his place saves a great deal of social divisiveness, for once he has done so the threat gesture suffices to establish precedence – though in comparison with the matriarchal hierarchy the bull hierarchy is so amorphous that it scarcely qualifies for the term.

Although bull herds, sometimes of more than 100 animals, have frequently been reported – which accounts for the long-standing but erroneous belief that elephant herds are invariably led by old bulls – these are only transient assemblages, and not herds in the true sense. From the time they are ejected from the family unit, bulls lead more or less solitary lives. Nevertheless they are seldom far from other elephants, and their relationships consist of a continuous ebb and flow of casual associations. These associations are invariably brief, often lasting only a few hours before the individuals concerned drift

**Right:** The establishment of a hierarchy helps to avoid unnecessary conflict. An inferior greets a superior member of the hierarchy by placing the tip of its trunk in the other's mouth.

**Right below:** Young bulls like to engage in friendly bouts of sparring. By testing their strength in this way a loose hierarchy is established.

**Opposite:** The mature bull leads a more or less solitary life. Lacking the advantages that go with being a member of a herd, he has to fend for himself.

apart again. There are no lasting male–female relationships. When a cow comes on heat, she has only a brief and very temporary association with a bull.

Mature bulls of equal status may fight for possession of a female on heat, though unmatched bulls still submit to the hierarchical rule that the inferior gives way. But even though several bulls may force their way into a family unit when one of its members comes on heat, fighting even among equals, is less common than might be supposed. The dominant bull takes precedence, but that does not prevent other bulls from mounting the cow during the three days or so during which she remains receptive.

Bulls past breeding age live almost like recluses. An old bull is often accompanied by one or more younger animals. Indeed, some experienced observers, among them

E. A. Temple-Perkins, an authority on the elephants of Uganda, insist that a really big bull invariably has an escort. Whether there is any significance to this companionship is another matter. It is widely believed that these self-appointed escorts attach themselves to the old bull to guard and protect him, but, in view of the bull elephant's characteristic disinclination to form close or lasting relationships with others of either sex, the probability is that these are merely chance associations of a purely temporary nature.

An aspect of elephant behaviour which has so far defied rational explanation is the bizarre practice of methodically covering corpses – not only of their own species but other animals and human beings as well – with branches, grass and other materials. Elephants also remove bones from the

skeletons of elephants lying in the bush, often carrying them hundreds of yards. Tusks seem to hold a particular fascination for them; they will carefully pull the tusks from their skull sockets and carry them in their trunks or mouths before smashing them against tree trunks or boulders, almost as though they were deliberately attempting to remove all trace of death. A. H. Neumann, one of the best-known professional elephant hunters at the turn of the century, was among the first to note this behaviour. He thought that it reflected the elephant's 'capacity for inferring possible danger to itself from the discovery of the remains of its own species'. As yet, no better theory has been offered in its place. The elephant is not, in fact, the only species to be alarmed or upset by the sight or scent of dead animals of its own kind.

# THE CULT OF THE ELEPHANT

Until man advanced beyond the level of the hunter food-gatherer, he had no cause even to attempt domestication of the elephant; not until mankind began to live in the settled communities which denoted the beginnings of civilization as we understand it was there any reason to think of doing so.

But this is not to suggest that the elephant had not figured indirectly in human affairs since before the dawn of history, long before being as it were drafted into human society. Rock paintings, some of which record events of 60,000 years ago, provide eloquent testimony to the man–elephant relationship in Stone Age society. Among the many fascinating examples of rock art featuring elephants is one from near Cathcart, in South Africa, showing a group of a dozen hunters hurling their spears at an encircled elephant; another at Cheke, in southern Tanzania, depicts an elephant surrounded by figures of people who appear to be vaulting over its back in a way reminiscent of Minoan priestesses somersaulting over the horns of bulls.

Animals were depicted in cave art in the belief that the act of capturing their image would give the hunter a hold over the animal and thus enhance his prospects. Hunting was the dominant activity in Stone Age society, and as the elephant, by virtue of its bulk and by-products, was a prime quarry of the hunter, it is scarcely surprising that it was of special significance to early man. It is impossible to do more than guess at the rites that preceded the hunt or followed its successful conclusion; but, to judge from comparable rituals which persist in parts of Africa down to the present day, we can infer that they formed an important part of the

**Left: In Ceylon the elephant has long had an important role in the cultural life of the island, as it has in India and South East Asia (above). Wall painting from a house in Udaypur.**

**Overleaf: On ceremonial occasions elephants are gorgeously apparelled and decorated.**

social and religious life of the time. As man's very existence depended on his hunting prowess, observance of the ceremonies to placate the spirits of the dead beast and, through prayers and offerings, to invoke its good will for future hunting successes was of supreme importance.

The advance of civilization led to hunting becoming more sophisticated. From being merely a necessary means of obtaining food, hunting became a form of recreation. If often combined sport with the military training that was so essential a feature of the times.

The early Middle Eastern monarchs looked upon hunting as their principal form of recreation and the hunting of certain species was reserved exclusively to royalty. To pit one's skill against the largest, the most ferocious or the swiftest animals was held to be a noble occupation, fit only for those of the highest rank. Elephant, lion, wild ass, bear, fallow deer and ostrich–each of which was at one time plentiful in Asia Minor–were among the animals hunted. One of the earliest records of elephant-hunting relates to the Pharaoh Thothmes III, the conqueror of Syria, who in 1464 BC had a narrow escape from a charging elephant while hunting in the Euphrates Valley.

It is easy to see how the early hunters' attitude towards their prey led by natural progression to the elephant being invested with an aura of mysticism. The elephant unquestionably had a prominent place in the early animistic and naturalistic cults, which attributed a spirit to almost every animate and inanimate object. From there it was only a step to its introduction into religious beliefs.

The cult of the elephant was deeply grounded in both Hinduism and Buddhism, as can be seen from the animal's representation in innumerable sculptures and stone reliefs, many of them masterpieces of Oriental art, in and around almost every temple and building of importance in India. The elephant also figures prominently in Indian mythology.

The Aryan invaders who moved into north-western India from Iran between 3000–1500 BC first occupied the upper Indus and its tributaries–the land of the five rivers. The fusion of the light-skinned Aryans with the earlier inhabitants of the Punjab– the dark-skinned Dravidians and the more primitive negroid tribes related to the Australian aborigines–led to a mixture of cultures and religious beliefs. Thus, although Indian mythology is founded upon the sacred Aryan scriptures–the Vedas–it contains elements of several distinctive cultures, including an infusion of Mongolian beliefs, which have become blended together in a complex, and often confusing, amalgam.

Chief of the early Vedic deities was Indra, who has many seemingly unrelated functions, combining divine attributes with human failings. He is at once Svargapati, lord of heaven; Vajri, god of thunder; and Meg-havahana, knight of the clouds. Not only is he the god of war and of the warrior caste but the symbol of fertility and scourge of the malevolent forces of Nature. When depicted with four arms–sometimes he has only two– one holds a bow, another an arrow-like thunderbolt, and the other two elephant goads. By hurling his bolts through the heavens, he triumphs over the turbulent clouds, forcing them to yield their contents and cast their water over the land. His lightning also sunders mountains and causes

torrents to pour forth, filling rivers with life-giving water and spilling onto the parched earth.

Indra lives on Mount Meru, the Asiatic Olympus, somewhere to the north of the Himalayas and reputedly midway between heaven and earth. There, amidst the swirling clouds, he and his queen Indrani are accompanied by the voluptuous Apsaras, or celestial dancers, and Gandharvas, the dissolute musicians who partner them. Sharing this paradise are groups of heroic warriors. Indra is usually depicted mounted on his celestial white elephant, Airavata, possessed of four tusks and born of the churning of the primeval ocean. Airavata is the reputed ancestor of all the elephants.

The churning of the oceans is one of the best-known sagas in Indian mythology. Indra, lord of the heavens, had a curse put on him which caused his powers to decline. Vishnu, the supreme god, offered to restore his strength provided that he undertook the monumental task of churning the primordial sea of milk to produce the nectar of immortality. To achieve this he had to use Mount Mandara, Vishnu's heavenly abode, as a gigantic twizzle-stick and Vasuki, king of the snakes, as a cord. This could be done only by enlisting the help of the demons, implacable enemies of the forces of enlightenment.

With the snake's body coiled around the mountain, the gods pulling at its tail and the demons at its head, the mountain revolved like a top so violently that the heat generated by its gyrations destroyed not only the mountain's own wildlife but the creatures of the ocean as well. Indeed, the mountain itself would have been destroyed had it not been for Indra who in the nick of time doused the flames with a cloudburst. By then the mountain was rotating at such speed that it was boring into the earth and seemed likely to cut right through. Vishnu, with great presence of mind, had the inspiration to transform himself into a huge turtle which burrowed beneath the spinning mountain and prevented it from going deeper.

Meanwhile, the gods and demons hauled on their snake rope with redoubled vigour. The snake, not surprisingly, fared none too well from this arrangement: overcome with the most appalling nausea, he spewed a veritable cascade of venom from his fangs, in such prodigious quantity that it swept over the earth like a tidal wave; gods and demons, men and animals, all were on the point of being engulfed. Fortunately, Shiva, hearing their desperate entreaties, sucked up the poison and the world was saved.

Then the sea of milk began to yield up its bounty. First to emerge was Kamadhenu, the fabulous cow of plenty, source of all life. She was followed by a galaxy of goddesses and Apsaras; and by Parijata, the tree of paradise, whose fragrance permeated the whole world. The moon came next, to be promptly expropriated by Shiva for wearing as a sacred emblem on his forehead. Finally came Lakshimi, goddess of prosperity, crowned with a garland of everlasting blooms and seated on a lotus. The sacred rivers implored her to immerse herself in their waters, while the four sacred elephants who bear the earth on their backs annointed her with water from the holy Ganges.

At length there emerged from the boiling cauldron of the sea the cup of immortality. The demons at once grabbed the precious nectar and fled. Vishnu's presence of mind

Left: Early man hunted the elephant mainly for food, as this graphic cave painting shows.

Opposite: The elephant figures prominently in Asiatic religion and mythology. The triumph of Hinduism over Buddhism is here symbolized by this twelfth-century representation of the lion's victory over the elephant.

Below: Elephants had a conspicuous place in the culture and economy of the Khmer Empire, both as working animals and for military purposes. These stone reliefs are a notable feature at Angkor Thom, Cambodia.

once again saved the situation: transforming himself into an entrancing woman, he diverted the demons' attention sufficiently to recover the ambrosia and return it to the gods. By drinking it their vigour was at once restored, whereupon they drove the demons away.

One of the most lively renderings of this famous legend is incorporated into the balustrade of the causeway leading to the entrance to Angkor Thom, the Cambodian capital of the Khmer Empire. Gods on one side of the balustrade, demons on the other, clasp their arms around the writhing body of the *naga*, the seven-headed snake. Passing between these two rows of grimacing figures, the visitor comes face to face with a group of elephant heads built into the gateway leading from the end of the causeway through the city wall.

Ganesha, the Hindu god of wisdom, good fortune and prudence, has the body of a man but the head of an elephant. The son of the goddess Parvati, he lost his original human head when he attempted to prevent Shiva from forcing his way into his mother's abode which it was Ganesha's responsibility to guard. Shiva, who as well as being the prince of demons was at the same time a benign deity, struck Ganesha's head from his shoulders. He then relented; but instead of restoring Ganesha's original head, ordained that he should be awarded the head of the first animal to appear. This, providentially, was an elephant.

Ganesha is always depicted with a pot belly and carrying a begging bowl in one hand. One evening he indulged so freely of the contents of his bowl that he felt constrained to ride off the effects of his meal.

Mounted on the rat which served as his normal steed, he was hacking along perhaps a trifle unsteadily by the light of the moon when his path was suddenly blocked by an immense snake. The rat was so terrified that it plunged off the path, throwing Ganesha with such force that his belly burst asunder.

Seizing the snake, Ganesha compelled it to make good the damage. No sooner was this done than the night sky was rent by the raucous sounds of uncontrollable mirth. Ganesha looked up to see the moon mocking him. In his fury, he tore out one of his tusks and hurled it with all his might at the moon. Since that moment the moon has been regularly deprived of a proportion of its light.

Ganesha is believed to be endowed with the intelligence of man and the sagacity of the elephant and it is therefore appropriate that he should be looked upon as the patron of literature and learning. In keeping with his elephantine temperament, he is of a calm and gentle disposition and a tower of commonsense and amiability – attributes which understandably make him one of the best-loved Hindu deities.

Guardian figures, in the form of elephants or other creatures, are frequently erected at the entrances to temples and sacred places. Their purpose is to assist the people to elevate their thoughts to the level required for religious observances. The animals chosen for this function are frequently the real or imaginary beasts of myth and legend, fit creatures to consort with the gods themselves. Enlisting animals of nobility and power as guardians has the dual function of paying respectful homage to the gods while at the same time warding off evil spirits.

The elephant above all other animals is considered particularly well endowed to uphold these virtuous aims. The high regard in which the elephant is held is nowhere seen to better advantage than at Kailasanatha, constructed on a site in Hyderabad closely associated with mythical gods and legendary heroes. This monumental temple bears witness not only to the ingenuity of its architects and builders but to their perseverance and patience, for it took more than a century to carve the columns and cloisters, the arches and gateways, the shrines and sanctuaries from the living rock. The entire temple complex is chiselled out of the mountainside. The principal sanctuary in the centre of this giant edifice is supported by eight pairs of elephants.

The practice of lining the approaches to sanctuaries with guardian figures was also followed in China, the supreme example being the Ming tombs, about 25 miles (40 kilometres) north of Peking. Known as the 'thirteen tombs', they are a fitting monument to the glories of the Ming Dynasty (1368–1644). Set among a broad valley in the hills, and interspersed among groves of sacred trees, are temples and towers, gateways and bridges, halls and courtyards, altars and tumuli. The entire complex is a masterpiece of Chinese artistry, skill and good taste; as much attention has been paid to the relationship of these exquisite buildings with the landscape in which they are sited as has been bestowed on the design and construction of the buildings themselves. The tombs are approached along a wide processional way flanked on either side by huge stone figures of warriors, mythological creatures and animals – horses, camels, lions and

elephants. At that time, the elephant was still to be found in parts of southern China, even though it was by then already becoming scarce.

In the east, above all in Thailand, a particular cult developed around the white elephant, to the extent that the animal came to be accorded all the attributes of divinity. White elephants are of course no more than albino elephants, differing only in their generally lighter coloration, pink eyes, patches of whitish skin, and 'gingery' hair. The degree of albinism varies from one individual to another, and a really pale skin is very rare.

A white elephant was regarded as so sacred that even the king himself was considered unworthy of mounting its back, and the animal would even be crowned to denote its sublime status. It was maintained in an appropriately exalted style, being provided with its own retinues of servants and slaves, spacious apartments, princely apparel, splendid jewellery and the finest food available. Musicians and minstrels heralded its approach, nobles made deep obeisance, and in taking its bath it was attended by a high-ranking officer bearing a huge umbrella of crimson and gold, deputed to shield its head, while courtiers annointed its body with fragrant perfumes and cooled it with golden fans. If captured young, it was customary for a white elephant calf to be suckled by a galaxy of human wet nurses. If it fell ill, the best physicians in the land were summoned to its side, while the chief priests chanted prayers in the temples and made offerings for its safe deliverance.

Although Islam does not encourage mythology and anthropomorphism, the humanization of animals, there is an Arabian story involving an elephant. An Ethiopian army under its general Abraha invaded Arabia with the declared purpose of destroying the Kaaba—Islam's most venerated shrine—but when the army arrived before Mecca, the elephant on which Abraha was riding sank to its knees and refused to rise, compelling the invaders to beat a hasty retreat.

In the East power and prestige were so closely bound up with the number of elephants at a ruler's command that the elephant naturally came to be regarded as the symbol of royal splendour, and figured prominently in the ceremonial of court and temple. The prescribed procedures followed in preparing it for these functions were very elaborate. After being bathed and anointed with fragrant perfumes, the animal's tusks were adorned with circlets of gold and auspicious markings were painted on its head and face. A golden diadem was placed upon its head, its neck decorated with golden chains and silken cords, and a cloak of royal purple edged with scarlet and gold was laid across its back. A host of attendants conducted it through the crowded streets, preceded by priests solemnly intoning its praises and musicians heralding its approach with fanfares of music; dancers and singers entertained for its benefit, and special plays were performed in its honour.

Although the elephant still participates in the ceremonial of great State occasions, the abolition of India's princely houses in 1970 has greatly reduced the opportunities for its use. The cult of the elephant—so much a part of India's cultural heritage—is therefore sadly on the wane.

The elephant symbolizes a past that is gone beyond recall; but its symbolism also reaches into the future. The elephant's future rests in our hands. If control of our own affairs has slipped so far from our grasp that we cannot find room on this planet for the elephant, it is a clear indication that we are running out of room for ourselves.

**Above: Ceremonial elephant in marble, Benares.**

**Right: Gigantic stone elephants are among the animals lining the approaches to the Ming Tombs, near Peking.**

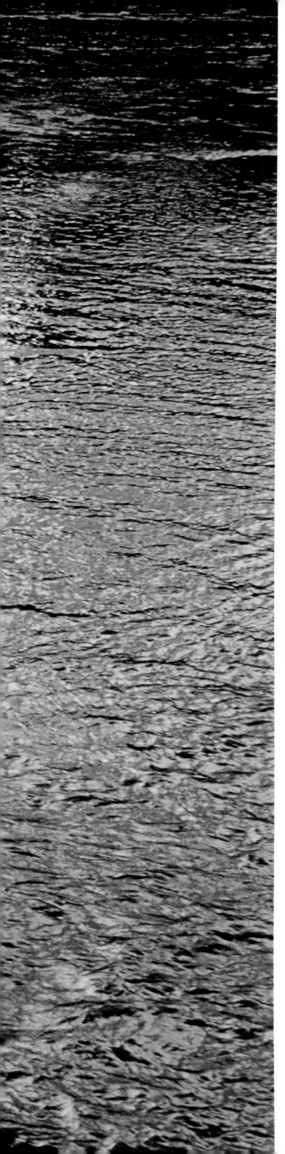

# THE ELEPHANT AND MAN

To primitive man the elephant must have seemed the embodiment of physical might. The animal's size and prodigious strength clearly excited the imagination of our remote ancestors and must have caused them to wonder how that intrinsic power could be harnessed to their own advantage. It is one thing to have the idea, quite another to put it into practice, and we can only admire their sheer temerity in deciding to subjugate the largest land animal in the world.

Exactly where or when the first attempts at domestication were made is not known. The earliest evidence so far unearthed are the seals excavated from the city of Mohenjodaro, which suggest that the elephant was domesticated at least as early as 1500 BC. Many of the seals – the only written record to have come down to us from this pre-Aryan Indus Valley civilization which flourished from about 2500–1500 BC – bear the representation of wild animals, among them rhinoceros, tiger and elephant. The elephant is depicted wearing what appears to be either saddlery or cloth of some kind, which implies that it was used for domestic purposes. Thus by the fourth century BC when Aristotle wrote his account of capturing elephants – the first mention of this subject in Western literature – it seems likely that the elephant had already been domesticated for at least 1000 years.

In those days elephants were probably captured in foot-snares, the method traditionally employed in Ceylon (now Sri Lanka) until the island's occupation by the Portuguese. The Portuguese, and later the Dutch, introduced and developed the *keddah*, or *kraal*, system of capturing elephants, which was quickly adopted by neighbouring countries and remains in wide use to this day. It involves driving wild elephants into a strongly built stockade constructed of stout baulks of timber. When a suitable herd is reported in the vicinity, long lines of beaters surround it on three sides, gradually shepherding it towards the keddah. A line of fences extending at about 45 degrees from either side of the keddah ensures that the

Left: At the end of the day's work the elephant is taken for its daily bath.

Above: Wall painting depicting Dev Tissa, who introduced Buddhism to Ceylon, supervising the ploughing of the land in preparation for the construction of the first stupa.

Above: Koonkies engaged in taming a newly captured elephant.

Opposite: Asiatic elephants have long been widely used for forestry work. These elephants, at Chieng Mai in northern Thailand, are carrying and stacking tree trunks.

elephants are channelled into the entrance. When the last animal has passed into the corral, tree trunks are dropped into position across the gate to block their escape.

It is essential that the stockade should contain water to attract the wild elephants into the pen, and stout trees to which they can be tied. Part of the beaters' function is to arrange the drive so that the herd is as far as possible denied access to water. Driving the herd has to be gradual so that the elephants' suspicions are not aroused – when they would almost certainly attempt to break out of the ring – and it is normally spread over several days; if the herd is at a great distance from the keddah, it may even take weeks. If all goes according to plan, therefore, the elephants reach the stockade with raging thirsts. The smell of water within the pen is then sufficient inducement for them to enter without demur. Sometimes sugarcane, an almost irresistible delicacy for an elephant, is used as an additional bait.

Once inside the keddah, the captives must be secured. The selected elephants are first cut out, one at a time, from the rest of the herd. Specially trained elephants, known as *koonkies*, are used and with the *mahout*, or trainer, rides an assistant who slides to the ground and, at the appropriate moment, slips a rope around the captive's foot. The elephants, especially cows with young calves, are by this time in a highly nervous state and milling around the stockade in their attempts to escape, so the nooser requires a cool nerve and perfect timing. He remains under cover of the koonkie's belly, and as his mount manoeuvres alongside the captive, he leaps out and gives the wild elephant's hind foot a sharp slap, making the animal raise its leg. As its foot comes clear of the ground he deftly slips the noose over it before dashing back to safety. The other end of the rope is attached to the koonkie. Any attempt at resistance is thwarted by koonkies closing in from either side; if necessary another pushes from the rear. Often, of course, the captive refuses to come quietly. If it sinks to the ground, koonkies force it to its feet. Surrounded and hemmed in, squeezed and shoved, the animal is propelled towards a tree to which it is firmly shackled.

After several days, when the captives have quietened down, each is firmly roped between two tame elephants and escorted to the training school. There it is allotted its own mahout, who from then on works exclusively with that particular animal and no other.

The trainee elephant is first yoked between

heavy poles and left without food or water. After a few days the mahout begins little by little to give it something to eat and drink . . and to spray it with water to relieve the bites of the innumerable flies which are by then plaguing the animal almost beyond endurance. The elephant responds to these attentions and soon allows itself to be touched. When that stage has been reached the process of training can begin. The captive is taken outside, once more sandwiched between a pair of koonkies, to learn to accept being handled. At first the animal reacts to being constantly touched and rubbed by attempting to defend itself with its trunk, but every time it does so the trainer, standing immediately in front of it, jabs the trunk with the point of his lance. Before long its trunk becomes so sore that the animal desists. After a few weeks comes the climax of its training: the mahout mounts for the first time, sliding into place around the animal's neck from the back of a koonkie. By then the mere sight of the goad – or *ankus* as it is usually called – is sufficient to overcome any lingering objection that might remain in the captive's mind. It is then only a short step to learning to obey the signals and commands of its mahout.

Although the keddah system is the normal method for mass captures, the pitfall is still used in some places for taking single animals. The pit is constructed in such a way that an elephant falling into it becomes so tightly jammed in the hole that it is unable to budge. To remove the animal from the pit, it is roped to a koonkie while logs or bundles of faggots are thrown in to raise the level of the floor. The disadvantage of this method is the danger of injury to the captive as it crashes into the pit.

Breeding among captive elephants is generally discouraged. This is because the cow is unable to work for a long period during the latter part of her lengthy gestation and between birth and weaning. Not only does the cow herself have to be kept during this otherwise unproductive period, there is also the heavy cost of maintaining the calf from birth to adolescence. For these reasons replacements are usually obtained from the wild. The aim is to catch adolescent animals, between fifteen and twenty years of age. At this age they can be put to work as soon as they have been trained, which seldom requires more than two months.

This explains why captive breeding of elephants has not been attempted in Sri Lanka and other countries where the abundance of free-living elephants serves as a reservoir from which replacements can be

drawn at will. But in Burma and the Indian states of Assam, Madras and Mysore the decline of the wild elephant and the consequent difficulty of obtaining replacements has stimulated the development of captive breeding.

In spite of their great size and strength, elephants are unable to carry heavy loads on their backs; there is therefore no point in using them as pack animals. But for lifting, pushing and hauling they are supreme, and it is for these tasks that they are primarily employed. On occasion they have been used on a huge scale: in the construction of Cambodia's famed temple at Angkor Wat the work force is said to have included 20,000 elephants.

Elephants continue to be used extensively in forestry work. They are employed not only in felling trees, which they do by simply pushing against the tree with the upper part of their trunk or forehead, they also drag the felled trees from the interior of the forest to assembly points. For hauling logs a single elephant is normally used; though for heavier logs a pair of elephants works in tandem. They are trained to stack the logs at the collecting point, lifting each one from the ground by sliding their tusks underneath and holding it in place with their trunk. But even in Burma, where the elephant has long been an almost integral part of the timber industry, the number of elephants working in the teak forests has declined by 75 per cent in the last forty years—from 6,000 in 1938 to 1,500 today.

Although unsuitable as pack animals—a task to which other animals are better adapted—elephants are frequently used for carrying people, either for ceremonial or hunting purposes or, a more modern innovation, for carrying tourists. The passenger rides in a *char-jarma*, a long wooden structure placed across the elephant's back, resting on a thickly padded 'saddle cloth' and held in place by leather girths. This is a popular form of transport in some of India's national parks where—at Kanha, for example—visitors are taken to see rhinos from the backs of elephants. There is always the possibility that the tourist may get a greater thrill than he bargained for: the Asiatic elephant's natural fear of the tiger is equalled only by its dislike of the great Indian rhinoceros. Rhinos, particularly females with young, have little hesitation in charging elephants, sometimes using their tusks with great effect to inflict severe gashes on legs, flanks or trunk.

When used for hunting, the elephant carries a *howdah*—resembling an outsize basket made of wood or wickerwork—strapped to its back. The howdah gives the hunter a vantage point from which he has an uninterrupted view all around—an important consideration in country where the quarry, usually tiger, lies up in dense vegetation.

But it was above all in the military sphere that the elephant excelled in the service of man. In much of Asia the elephant was for centuries the dominant animal on the battlefield. Exactly when elephants were first used in war is uncertain, but it seems reasonable to assume that even if domestication was not originally undertaken primarily for that purpose, their use in war must have quickly followed. Certainly the Assyrians knew of war elephants, even if they did not themselves possess them: the Assyrian queen Semiramis resorted to using dummy elephants—straw-filled skins mounted on camels—when she invaded India in the ninth century BC.

Until the invention of gunpowder, a squadron of elephants, protected by armour either of sheet metal or fire-hardened leather, and carrying a posse of archers and other men-at-arms, was an extremely formidable adversary. War elephants were effective less perhaps for their fighting qualities than for their psychological impact on enemy infantry and cavalry: horses become terrified in the presence of elephants. The demoralizing effect of a task force of elephants opposing an enemy equipped only with hand weapons can be imagined. The effect was much the same, to draw a modern parallel, as you would expect from exposing riflemen to attack by armoured tanks. The commander fielding the largest contingent of elephants would naturally be at a tremendous advantage. It is not surprising that the elephant came to be regarded as the embodiment of power, or that a monarch's prestige was assessed according to the number of war elephants in his stable.

Marco Polo relates how Kublai Khan, Emperor of China, was carried into battle in a wooden 'castle' mounted on the backs of a team of four elephants. When the Huns invaded northern India, their forces, according to a contemporary Chinese account, included '700 war elephants, each of which carries ten men armed with swords and spears, while the elephants are armed with swords attached to their trunks, with which they fight at close quarters'.

There were occasions when elephants were used on a massive scale. During the siege of Colombo in 1587, for instance, the Sinhalese were said to have deployed a force of 2,200 war elephants against the Portuguese.

Even a solitary war elephant could be highly effective, as shown during Caesar's invasion of Britain in 54 BC. Sir Gavin de Beer describes how 'Caesar wanted to cross the Thames, which Cassivelaunus, King of the Britons, fought to prevent with many horsemen and chariots. But in his army Caesar had something which the Britons had never seen before: a huge elephant, protected with iron armour and bearing on its back a tower in which were archers and slingsmen, who were ordered to advance across the river. The Britons were terrified at the sight of such an outsize animal, against which horses were unavailing. For as in the case of the Greeks, horses bolted at the bare sight of an elephant. Nor could the Britons stand up to this armoured fighting animal possessed of fire-power and shooting arrows and sling-stones at them. With their horses and their chariots they turned and fled, and the Romans were able to cross the Thames without danger because their enemies took fright at one animal. An elephant and castle.'

Thanks to the Greek historian Arrian, the most graphic account to have come down to us is of Alexander the Great's famous battle of the Jhelum, or Hydaspes, fought in 326 BC. His antagonist, Porus, King of the Punjab fielded a large contingent of elephants. Alexander was already familiar with war elephants, having encountered them during his earlier battles with Darius, King of the Persians, who had succeeded in acquiring a contingent. Nevertheless the psychological impact on the Macedonian troops, their morale already at a low ebb, must have been very great.

On approaching the Indus, Alexander took the precaution of sending out patrols with specific instructions to scour the countryside for information about elephants. He even managed to acquire thirteen which had been abandoned by the Indians. These made a valuable addition to his force: he already possessed 25 elephants presented by the rajah of Taxila, who looked to Alexander for aid against his more powerful neighbour.

With the Jhelum River swollen by monsoon rains, Alexander's best hope of crossing lay in fording the river at Haranpur. But Porus, reckoning on this possibility, had taken the precaution of guarding the ford with a strong force which, in addition to archers and chariots, included 85 elephants. Realizing that to attempt to force the river in the teeth of such powerful opposition would be courting disaster, Alexander sought and eventually found an alternative crossing at Jalalpur, 17 miles (27·4 kilometres) farther up stream.

**Although the number of working elephants is declining, they are very popular for carrying visitors.**

When word reached him that the rajah of Kashmir was advancing to Porus's support, Alexander acted without further delay. In a surprise night assault under cover of a torrential thunderstorm, he crossed the river at Jalalpur with a substantial force, established a bridgehead, and advanced on Porus.

Porus's army included about 130 elephants, in addition to the 85 guarding Haranpur. He stationed them in an extended line immediately in front of his infantry, with his cavalry and chariots on either flank. Alexander gained his victory by the sheer brilliance of his tactics. At the height of the battle, with his main cavalry force already deeply committed, Porus, directing the fight from his huge elephant, was appalled to see two divisions of Macedonian cavalry whose existence he had not suspected tearing into the rear of his army.

Peter Green, in his book *Alexander the Great*, gives a graphic account of the battle and of how the Macedonian forces came to grips with Porus's elephants: 'The real nightmare facing the phalanx – one that haunted them for the rest of their days – was that row of maddened, trumpeting, furious elephants. Alexander had worked out a technique for dealing with these beasts: encircle them, let the archers pick off their mahouts, and then discharge volleys of javelins and spears into the most vulnerable parts of their anatomy. The infantrymen, meanwhile, slashed through their trunks with Persian scimitars, or chopped at their feet with axes. The elephants had several very effective tricks of their own. Some Macedonian soldiers they stamped underfoot, crushing them to a bloody pulp, armour and all. Others they caught up with their trunks and dashed to the ground. Others, again, found themselves impaled on the great beasts' tusks. As Porus's squadrons were pressed back, the elephants, hemmed in a narrowing space, began to trample their own side: the cavalry suffered particularly heavy losses because of them. . . . This frightful struggle left its mark on Alexander's men. Their nerve, if not broken, was severely shaken; and nothing Alexander said or did would ever reconcile them to facing elephants in battle again.'

Half a century after Alexander's death, the Carthaginians began to train the African forest elephant, which they obtained from Tunisia, Algeria and Morocco. According to Sir William Gowers, in his account of *The African Elephant in History*, the Carthaginian training programme started in 277 BC. The forest elephant saw wide service during the Punic Wars, the most famous occasion being Hannibal's renowned crossing of the Alps in 218 BC. By taking his army through the Alps, Hannibal outflanked the Roman defences and attacked Italy from the least expected quarter. Hannibal was one of the outstanding men of history; yet it is a strange reflection on our sense of values that he should be remembered less for his unsurpassed military brilliance which enabled him to maintain a Carthaginian army on Roman soil for fifteen years, less for his inspired and inspiring leadership which surmounted every obstacle and led his mercenary forces to victory after victory over the finest Roman generals of the day, less for his unwavering courage and his constancy to the Carthaginian cause despite tardy support from his homeland, than he is for having trekked 37 elephants over the Alps.

After Hannibal's defeat by Scipio Africanus at the battle of Zama in 202 BC, the Carthaginians were obliged not only to give up all their war elephants but never again to train more.

Two thousand years elapsed before any further attempt was made to domesticate the African elephant. In 1899, the Belgians opened an establishment in the Congo. The elephant training school at Gangala-na-Bodio continues to this day, but the African elephant is much more difficult to train than the Indian, and results are limited in comparison with those obtained with the Asiatic species.

The Director of the Tanzania National Parks has nevertheless expressed the hope that trained African elephants will in future be used to transport visitors through the proposed Mahari Mountains National Park, situated on the eastern shore of Lake Tanganyika, which will shortly be set aside as a chimpanzee sanctuary. One can only hope that this is not indicative of the elephant's future role in the national parks of East Africa.

**Above: The Asiatic elephant's natural fear of the tiger has been overcome in this circus act.**

**Top: Specially trained elephants have long been used for hunting. This drawing, dating from 1819, depicts a leopard hunt.**

**Right: An illustration from the Akbar-Nama manuscript, dated about 1590, now in the Victoria & Albert Museum. Akbar's elephant Hawai breaks down the bridge of boats across the Jumna River pursuing another elephant Ran Bagha.**

**Overleaf: The African forest elephant is more suitable for domestication than the bush elephant, although neither is as amenable as the Asiatic elephant.**

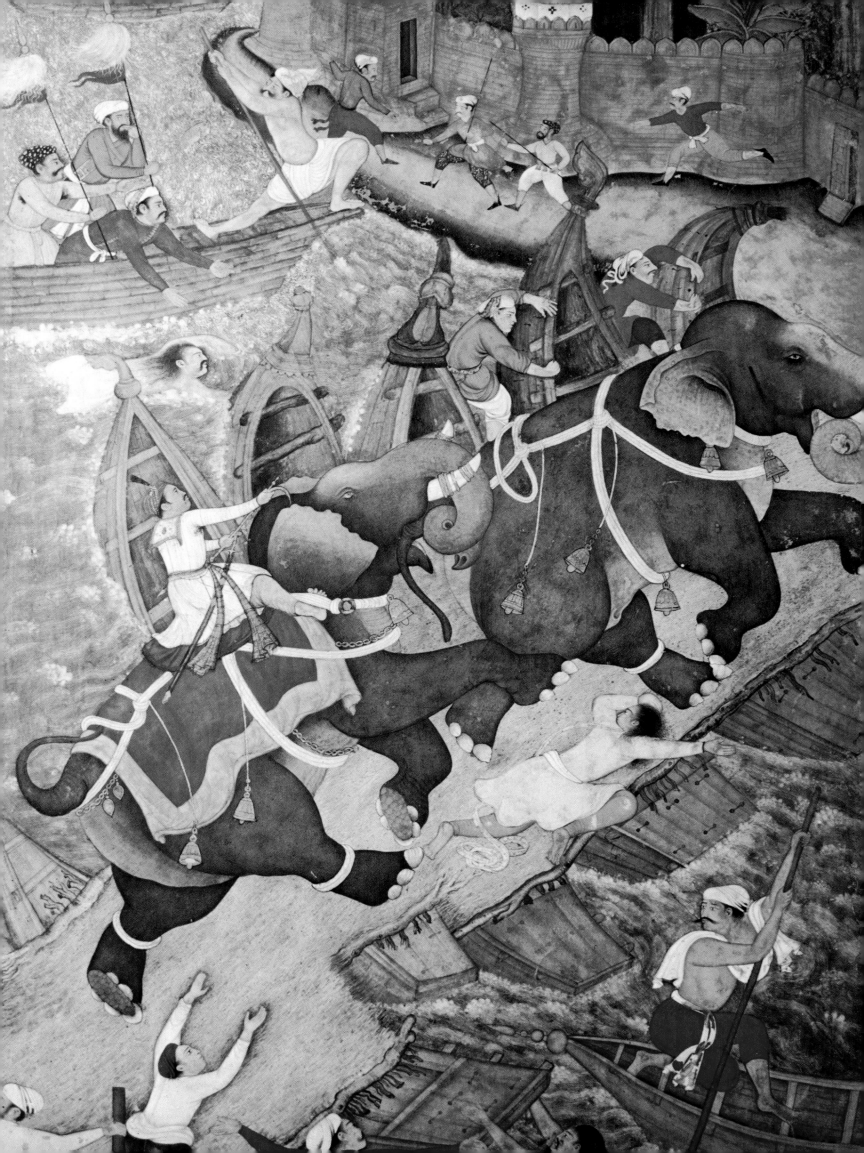

# THE IVORY TRADE

The demand for ivory is as old as man himself. It is an exceptionally hard substance, but despite being difficult to cut and work, it is highly valued in the manufacture of tools and implements and for ornamentation. It is an ideal medium for carving and has for centuries been used for this purpose, principally in the East but also around the Mediterranean and in parts of West Africa.

The oldest ivory carvings are a group of small figurines carved by Aurignacian mammoth hunters more than 20,000 years ago, almost certainly for use in propitiation ceremonies. Perhaps the most remarkable ivory carving of antiquity was the statue of Athene, the creation of the celebrated sculptor Phidias, which was housed in the Parthenon. It stood almost 40 feet (12·2 metres) high. The drapery was rendered in gold but the face, arms and hands were of ivory, a combination long favoured by the Greeks but never previously employed on such a scale. As even the largest tusk cannot yield a slab of ivory more than about 30 inches (533 millimetres) long and 6 inches (152 millimetres) wide, the question has often been asked whether the ancient Greeks knew a special method of processing ivory into larger sheets than could be obtained from any tusk.

Because of its superior size and quality, African ivory was preferred to Asiatic. Thus, long before the interior of Africa first became known to the Western world – and in eastern and central Africa this occurred only about 100 years ago – ivory had been one of Africa's

two main exports, the other being slaves.

Part of the almost insatiable demand for African ivory was originally met from North Africa. But by the end of the great Islamic conquests in the seventh century AD, the elephant had for all practical purposes ceased to exist in North Africa. Enterprising traders were therefore obliged to look farther

**Left: Ivory has been used for carving since before the dawn of history. Its popularity has not diminished over the years. An ivory carver at work in Zaire.**

**Above: Ivory chesspiece, depicting the days of the Raj in India.**

south for their supplies. Trading posts established at many points around the coast of Africa obtained both ivory and slaves from tribal chiefs and petty kings living in the unknown interior. These two items – 'black' and white ivory – were for centuries the principal items of African commerce: there was little else which the local people could barter for the cloth, beads and other manufactured goods for which they hankered. As recently as 1891, the recognized exchange rate in the neighbourhood of Mount Elgon was six strings of beads for one 16-pound (7·3 kilogram) tusk.

Thus, many years before the Portuguese, inspired by the vision of Prince Henry the Navigator, ventured down the west coast of Africa, the Arabs had already gained a monopoly of the east coast ivory trade. Long columns of slaves carrying tusks on their heads wound their way from the interior to Arab settlements at the coast where both 'black' and white ivory were sold; dhows riding on the monsoon transported both commodities to distant lands. Much of the ivory went to Arabia and India; some went as far as China, for the discovery of large amounts of Chinese porcelain along the coast of East Africa from Somalia to Madagascar, much of it dating from the fourteenth century, indicates long-established connections with China. Thus, for many years before the arrival off Mombasa and Malindi of the Portuguese caravels in the fifteenth century, Chinese junks had been regularly plying to the ancient Arab cities scattered along the East African seaboard in quest of ivory and rhinoceros horn.

It was a highly lucrative business. Tippu Tib, one of the best-known slave traders, returned from one safari with 68,250 pounds (27,329 kilograms) of ivory valued at £13,650 – an enormous sum in those days.

Further evidence of the huge profits to be derived from the ivory trade is given by Sir Samuel Baker. During his exploration of the southern Sudan he estimated that ivory yielded 'a minimum profit for the Government of 1500 per cent. A few beads, together with three or four gaudy-coloured cotton handkerchiefs, a zinc mirror, and a fourpenny butcher's knife, would purchase a tusk worth twenty or thirty pounds. I calculated expenses of transport from England, together with interest on capital. In some cases we purchased ivory at 2000 per cent profit, and both sellers and buyers felt perfectly contented.'

In Mozambique and Angola the slave trade was officially abolished in 1836, although another twenty years elapsed before slavery itself was legally outlawed; in Zanzibar the process took a little longer. Abolition in the Portuguese territories coincided with the lifting of the royal monopoly on ivory trading. This opened the way to a concerted slaughter of elephants, for one of the immediate practical results of stamping out slavery was to leave ivory as Africa's only commercially valuable commodity. African potentates, finding themselves suddenly deprived of their main source of revenue from 'black' ivory, compensated themselves by redoubling their efforts to obtain white.

Until then the Arabs had been content to wait at the coast for the delivery of consignments of slaves and ivory from the interior, purchasing them from African dealers and middlemen as they would any other merchandise. But the Arab's role now underwent a fundamental change: from being merchants

Left: The almost insatiable demand for ivory resulted in the elephant becoming a prime target for the hunter.

Top left: Mammoth tusks from Siberia on the ivory floor at the London Docks.

Top: As the elephants enter the keddah, a heavy door is lowered behind them to block their escape.

Above: An old print showing a newly captured elephant firmly roped to trees.

and traders living permanently at the coast, they began to move into the interior, in the process becoming ever more deeply involved in political and military activities. By allying themselves with one tribe against another, the well-armed Arabs turned inter-tribal warfare to their own advantage, and thus established themselves as the dominant force in the interior of Africa north of the Limpopo.

The Arabs also took advantage of this new situation to arm the local tribesmen with firearms to obtain ivory on their behalf. Some African hunters set themselves up independently. They combed the country for elephants, devastating the herds in one area before moving on to the next. Anarchy followed in their wake, for these gangs of marauding hunters became so powerful and tyrannical that they exterminated whole tribes, bringing devastation to a vast area.

An indication of the scale on which hunting was conducted can be gained from the large quantities of firearms acquired by African hunters. Official statistics for 1888, for instance, show 'that from 80,000 to 100,000 firearms of all kinds found their way annually into Africa through the eastern ports, and weapons of precision were rapidly supplementing the inferior and old-fashioned guns'. In the first six months of the same year, more than 69,000 pounds (31,296 kilograms) of gunpowder and 1,000,000 bullets were being imported into the territories administered by the Portuguese. These figures lend weight to Selous's contention that 'native Africans possessed of firearms . . . have been the principal factor in the destruction of game between the Limpopo and the Zambezi'.

Selous backed his assertion by describing the situation in Matabeleland. Until 1872

'there were many parts of the vast territory lying between the high plateaux of Matabeleland and Mashonaland and the Zambezi River where elephants had never yet been molested by a European or even by a native armed with a rifle. During the next three years, however, swarms of Lobengula's hunters, in addition to Europeans, killed most of the big tuskers in these hitherto untouched districts—during which period no less than 60,000 pounds [27,214 kilograms] weight of ivory was sold to traders by Lobengula; or, including the lowest estimate obtained by Europeans and their native hunters, the total obtained in the three years preceding 1875 must have reached 100,000 pounds [45,357 kilograms].'

South of the Limpopo the elephant had already been practically exterminated. By the 1860s all but a few pockets had gone. The

Boers were almost by definition hunters. Their life style forced them into self-sufficiency which involved living off the land and the game animals that were on it. Hunting became such an integral part of the pattern of their existence that in course of time it came to symbolize their way of life. The prodigal slaughter of wildlife in which they indulged was matched only by the whole-sale destruction of bison, pronghorn antelope and other native animals that was simultaneously taking place throughout the prairielands of North America. By the end of the nineteenth century the elephant had almost ceased to exist in the whole of South Africa.

Far to the north, Tippu Tib, who started his career as a Zanzibar merchant, was engaged in establishing a series of trading posts linked by regular caravan routes with the coast. His real name was Hamed bin Muhammed, but he acquired the native name by which he came to be generally known from an onomatopoeic rendering of the sound of musket fire–'Tip-tip-tib'.

It was Tippu Tib, perhaps more than any other individual, who opened up the interior of East Africa. His word was law over a huge area, and although it could be said that he exercised power without responsibility, it is nonetheless true that many European explorers and missionaries owe much, sometimes their very lives, to his assistance. Tippu Tib's interests lay not in geographic discovery but in trade, but his goodwill was a factor of supreme importance in the early exploration of east-central Africa and the discovery of the great inland lakes and the source of the Nile. Livingstone, Stanley and Speke were among those whom he helped.

**Above: The pastoral Masai are tradi-tionally tolerant of wildlife. This moran is carrying the tusk of an elephant killed by others.**

**Opposite: One of the simplest but most deadly weapons favoured by the modern poacher is the wire snare. Cheap and easy to instal, this fiendish device kills entirely indiscriminately.**

Another was von Wissmann, who made the first west to east crossing of the continent and later became Imperial Commissioner of German East Africa, now Tanzania.

Hermann von Wissmann, who has been described as 'one of the great men of Africa', was not only closely concerned with the creation of German East Africa and an outstanding administrator, he was also one of the most far-sighted conservationists of his day and instrumental in establishing Tanzania's first game reserves. Von Wissman's visits to the Congo in the 1880s when that region was under Tippu Tib's control had greatly impressed him with Tippu Tib's method of regulating the hunting of elephants: he imposed conditions whereby half of all ivory taken had to be surrendered to him. Von Wissmann believed that this held the germ of an idea which could be turned to the advantage of conservation by the simple expedient of making the tribe, through its chief, responsible for the prevention of hunting by any outsider. The tribe would be compensated by some special privilege or, alternatively, certain authorized members of the tribe would be permitted to shoot a limited number of elephants for their own use. In this way, he reasoned, the wildlife sanctuaries would be effectively protected by the tribesmen themselves, as it would be in their own interests to do so. Von Wissmann's proposal was echoed by the British Colonial Office, which observed that 'the native chiefs should also be given a pecuniary interest in the preservation of game as well as in the enforcement of the game laws'. Unfortunately, these ideas, being far ahead of their time, were not adopted. If they had been, and the tribesmen directly concerned brought into a form of partnership with the authorities, the subsequent story of wildlife conservation in Africa might have been along very different lines.

The method favoured by more orthodox minds was to set aside strictly protected game reserves in which tribal hunting was rigorously outlawed. This caused such resentment among the Africans, who derived no benefit from the arrangement, that they became openly and vociferously hostile to the whole concept of wildlife conservation, seeing it simply as a device for depriving them of their traditional hunting rights.

After the formal declaration of the East Africa Protectorate in 1895, the government officers charged with responsibility for administering the territory on the shoe-string sums allotted by a parsimonious Parliament at Westminster, sought to supplement the country's revenues by encouraging Europeans to visit the country either as sportsmen or, on a more permanent basis, as settlers.

For sportsmen ivory was of course the prime attraction—not only was a pair of 100-pound (45-kilogram) tusks the hunter's supreme trophy, ivory was almost the only commercially valuable commodity to be derived from hunting. And as the mounting of a foot safari—in which it was nothing out of the ordinary to employ several hundred porters for a period of months, sometimes even years—was an extremely expensive undertaking, all but a few sportsmen found it necessary to offset part of the heavy costs through the sale of ivory.

Between the time of abolition and the construction of the railway from Mombasa to Lake Victoria ivory was, moreover, the only natural produce sufficiently valuable to stand the heavy cost of transportation. Porters had to be employed to undertake the work previously performed by slaves; and human porterage from the interior to the coast cost approximately £300 a ton.

The opening of the railway—the line reached Nairobi in 1899—completely altered this situation. The freight charges on ivory sent by rail were so cheap in comparison with human porterage that the profit on ivory once more soared to astronomical heights. Traders—mainly Indians—did everything they could to take advantage of this favourable state of affairs by encouraging tribesmen to hunt for them.

Among the native hunters who responded to this call were many Wakamba, members of a Kenya tribe living close to what is now the Tsavo National Park. The Wakamba had for long been accustomed to trading in ivory. Each year as soon as their crops were safely harvested, parties of warriors, usually several hundred strong, set off on elephant hunting forays lasting anything up to three months. During this time they lived off the country: apart from his weapons, each man carried only a bag of ground millet to supplement his diet of game meat. These tough warriors ranged over an immense area, reaching as far as the coast; they did not hesitate to harry and plunder as they went. The Galla and other tribesmen living along the Tana River went in constant fear of their lives, and at least one small tribe—the Mumoniot—is known to have been annihilated by Wakamba warriors.

The extension of the railway to Kampala naturally helped to tap the substantial ivory resources of Uganda. Ivory had long been an important item in the revenues of that country. When Sir Samuel Baker explored the upper reaches of the Nile in the 1860s he found Mutesa, the powerful Kabaka of Uganda, carrying on a thriving trade in ivory. Mutesa was one of the few African rulers to prove too strong for the Arabs to manipulate, but there was mutual advantage in trading Mutesa's ivory for 'cotton stuffs, silks, guns and powder, brass-coil bracelets, beads, etc. The beads were exchanged by equal weight for ivory'.

The lure of quick and substantial profit led a few Europeans to adopt ivory hunting as a way of life, albeit a tough and uncertain one. One of the best known of the professional ivory hunters was Karamoja Bell; for years he hunted elephants in the remoter parts of East Africa, some of which remain relatively little known even today. But although some individual bags were spectacular, the tally of elephants shot by professional ivory hunters was officially stated to be 'trifling compared with the vast numbers which are constantly being mobbed and followed and killed by natives'. This assertion was reinforced by the fact that in 1896 at Moshi, then in German East Africa, now Tanzania, Africans were 'cheerfully paying 500 rupees [a considerable sum in those days] for permission to hunt elephants'.

The demand for ivory remains as great as ever, for no wholly satisfactory artificial substitute has ever been found. In recent years the market value of ivory has increased tenfold, with the inevitable result that illicit hunting has reached an unprecedented level. Today, almost the only areas in which the elephant can live unmolested are the national parks and game reserves which have been established for the explicit purpose of providing true sanctuary.

**Above: Tippu Tib.**

**Opposite: Indo-Portuguese ivory carving depicting the Good Shepherd, dated seventeenth or eighteenth century.**

# THE ELEPHANT'S FUTURE

Wildlife conservation in Africa started with the elephant. At the time when serious thought was first given to conserving the continent's native fauna, the elephant was both widespread and abundant, and one might have thought it was in little need of protection. But, viewed against the background of the ivory trade, it is not altogether surprising that, even before the establishment of the East Africa Protectorate had been officially proclaimed, fears were already being expressed that the slaughter of wildlife, and above all elephants, was being conducted on a scale that could not long be sustained. A few far-sighted individuals, among them Hermann von Wissmann and Sir Harry Johnston, the Special Commissioner in Uganda, began to press for the establishment of game reserves and, a little later, to secure the support of their governments in convening an international conference, held in London in May 1900, with the aim of protecting the fauna of the territories controlled by the signatories 'from the destruction which has overtaken wild animals in Southern Africa and other parts of the globe'.

But even the most dedicated supporters of East Africa's first game reserves recognized that while the reserves would be invaluable in protecting the more sedentary types of animals, they would be of only marginal help to the elephant. The seasonal movements of the elephant herds in their constant search for fodder and water took them over areas too vast to be contained within the boundaries of any reserve that it would be practical to envisage. Elephants also regularly migrated across international frontiers into adjacent territories, making it

Left: Elephants are one of the prime attractions of the great national parks of Africa.

Above: Tourists on the way to the Murchison Falls by boat frequently have close-up views of elephants.

necessary to have a common policy on both
sides of the frontier. The problem of year-
round containment of elephants within the
confines of a reserve is still with us today –
still without any satisfactory solution.

Quite apart from these considerations,
the sheer magnitude of the problem of administering the reserves was formidable.
And unless they were efficiently administered
they would serve no useful purpose: indeed,
they would be worse than useless for they
would give the misleading impression that
constructive action had been taken when in
fact it had not.

At that time the general consensus of in-
formed opinion was that the elephant would
inevitably be exterminated except in areas
such as the forests of the Congo Basin where
large herds could remain unmolested; because of their remoteness and difficulty of
access, these areas were in effect vast natural
sanctuaries.

The original range of the African elephant
was very extensive, covering the greater
part of the continent, including at one time,
what is now the Sahara. Until about 6000–
5000 BC the Sahara was a relatively well-
watered region inhabited by most of the
species associated with grassland savannas.
Evidence of these long-vanished herds has

**Top right: A family unit in Tanzania's
Manyara National Park.**

**Below right: Elephants in Uganda's
Murchison Falls National Park have
become accustomed to passing tourists.**

come to us through the marvellously vivid sequences of rock paintings in the Tassili Mountains and other parts of the great desert.

As the rate of rainfall decreased and the Sahara entered its present dry phase, elephants could survive only around its outer fringes; by early historical times they had disappeared from the whole of northern Africa except the north-west and the upper reaches of the Nile and its tributaries.

In Roman times elephants were still to be found in the forested foothills of the Atlas Mountains in the north-western corner of Africa. In the intervening two thousand years, and more particularly during the last century, the range of the African elephant has contracted substantially. The animal has virtually vanished from both the northern and southern extremities of its range. A tiny remnant living precariously in Mauritania is all that now remains of the north-western herds, and an even smaller herd living under intensive protection in the Addo National Park is all that remains to remind us that elephants once roamed over Cape Province.

Elsewhere the status of the elephant is only a little less precarious. The large herds that once existed in West Africa, for example, have steadily diminished under unremitting pressure from a constantly expanding human population with an insatiable craving both for land and for 'bush meat'. The more land taken up for agriculture and other forms of human development, the less there is for wildlife, and every reduction of habitat is inevitably followed by an intensification of hunting pressure on the areas that remain. In West Africa there are a large number of so-called 'professional hunters' who earn their living by selling game meat. Every town or village market has its quota of stalls doing a thriving trade in 'bush meat'.

The largest concentrations of elephants surviving today are to be found in the Nile drainage system, particularly in and around the Sudd, the wide-spreading papyrus swamps covering an area of about 100,000 square miles (25,900,000 hectares) in the southern Sudan. These almost impenetrable swamps are surrounded by extensive savanna lands which become inundated during the rainy season, providing the elephant with a vast natural sanctuary.

Elephants from this great natural reservoir overflow into adjacent regions, and in parts of Uganda the density of elephants is greater than any other part of East Africa. The Uganda Game Department, like the Game Departments of the other East African territories, was originally established to control game, above all to control elephants. On the basis of an estimated population of 25,000 elephants, the Game Department considered it necessary to shoot an average of 2,300 a year merely to keep the overall total from increasing.

Although there are fewer elephants in Africa today than in the past, overcrowding is, paradoxically, a greater problem than ever before. Although sanctuaries have been created specifically for the elephant's protection, few of them are self-contained to the extent that they are not affected by pressures from the outside world.

Even a relatively self-sufficient sanctuary such as Manyara is subject to influences and pressures from beyond its boundaries, some of which can have a profound effect. For example, game control measures in areas bordering the park can cause large numbers of animals to seek refuge there, creating a sudden surge in the animal population beyond the park's ability to support it.

With human pressures increasing around the boundaries of almost every national park, problems of this type inevitably become more frequent and more acute with the passage of time. South Africa's Kruger National Park offers an example of the over-

population likely to arise from the confinement of elephants. In 1931 the elephant population was about 135; since then numbers have grown – partly through immigration from nearby Mozambique – until by 1968 they exceeded 7,700. Part of the Kruger Park's boundary has to be marked by an elephant-proof fence, constructed of heavy wire cable, to keep elephants from wandering onto adjoining agricultural land. Other sanctuaries, in both Africa and Asia, have the same problem.

The confinement of wildlife populations within areas that are not ecologically self-sufficient creates 'unnatural' situations which have to be compensated for their ecological shortcomings. This calls for management. The more artificial the situation, the greater the degree of management required.

The notion of protection as an end in itself has gradually given way to the concept of carefully controlled management. For blanket protection is feasible only in areas that are ecologically self-sufficient, when Nature can be relied on to maintain her own equilibrium. Under such conditions the habitat itself exercises population control, determining the level of scarcity or abundance of the fauna.

The aim of wildlife management should therefore be the maintenance of the broad spectrum of plants and animals forming the natural community which, in combination, act and react upon each other to maintain a complicated conversion cycle. This is easy to state but infinitely difficult to put into practice. There is, for a start nothing static or rigid about a habitat and the animals and plants which occupy it; a natural community is a dynamic entity in process of constant change. The idea of management simply as a means of preserving an existing *status quo* is likely to be fruitless, for this would only conflict with the natural processes which it should be the aim of management to preserve.

The difficulty becomes highlighted when we turn to the problem of habitat 'damage'. As Sir Frank Fraser Darling and others have pointed out, the elephant is Nature's bulldozer. By uprooting trees, breaking through dense thickets, ripping down bush, and tearing up coarse vegetation, the elephant has the effect of stimulating the spread of plants which might not otherwise be able to grow and of opening up parts of the environment to other animals. They also play an important, sometimes an indispensible, part in seed dispersal. The seed of certain trees is unable to germinate in the close vicinity of the parent tree and needs an agent to disperse it. When the seed is exceptionally large – as, for example, the Borassus palm – the elephant is the only animal capable of swallowing it and thus distributing it in its droppings. Thus what at first sight appears to be damage may on closer investigation be regarded in an altogether different light; superficial damage may come to be recognized as either harmless or even beneficial.

Nature's system is to work in cycles, some extremely complex and few well understood. They involve the build-up, sometimes very rapid, of particular plant and animal populations under favourable conditions, followed sooner or later by a crash which inevitably happens when conditions cease to be favourable. Situations of this kind are well-known phenomena under undisturbed natural conditions – the swarming of lemmings is one of the most familiar examples – and it can be readily appreciated that there is an even greater tendency for them to occur in artificially contrived sanctuaries which do not meet the full ecological requirements of the animals they are supposed to protect. Nowhere is this dilemma seen more graphically than in Kenya's Tsavo National Park, which extends to more than 8,000 square miles (2,072,000 hectares) and contains larger populations of elephant and black rhinoceros than any other national park in the world.

The first sign that something unusual was happening came in the mid-1950s when elephants began deliberately stripping the bark from baobab trees. Using both tusks and trunk, they systematically tore off the bark from ground level to as high as they could reach, to get at the fibrous material underneath. This they chewed and spat out, leaving what looked like gigantic bird pellets scattered around the foot of the tree. By the time the elephants had finished, long strips of bark hung from the tree trunk like a shredded tunic. The damage was sometimes so great that a hole large enough to hold a man standing upright was bored right through the tree – a remarkable feat when you realize that mature baobabs commonly grow to a girth well in excess of 30 feet (9·1 metres). The effect of such extreme ring-barking is, of course, to kill the tree. Gradually the baobabs, which for as long as anyone could recall had been a prominent feature of the park, crashed to the ground. On at least one occasion an elephant standing underneath a damaged baobab was crushed and killed by its fall.

Tree damage by elephants is not peculiar to Tsavo; at Manyara, for instance, bark-shredding has caused many *Acacia tortilis* trees to wither and die. In the Serengeti elephants concentrated on the large *Acacia xanthophloea,* the yellow-barked fever trees fringing the water courses; their destruction converted the Acacia parkland into almost treeless grassland. Although the reason for the elephants attacking the trees is often associated with feeding, some trees are knocked over not for food but for some psychological reason, possibly caused by stress. Both sexes are known to indulge in this habit, though bulls seem more addicted to it than cows.

This stress behaviour is just one indicator of the 'Tsavo problem', which is essentially a conflict of opinion between those who wish to regulate the numbers of elephants in the reserve and those who would rather let Nature take its course. Quite apart from ethical considerations – large-scale killing being inconsistent with the aim of a national park – cropping elephants within the park could conceivably create as many difficulties as it might solve.

Essentially, the 'Tsavo problem' stems from the build-up of human pressures around the perimeter of the park compelling the elephants to remain within the protected area; as a result, the park's limited food supplies are not sufficient to support them. The anti-poaching campaign conducted by the Tsavo National Park's staff in the late 1950s, by suppressing illicit hunting in and around the park, may also have contributed to the increase of elephants. Whether or not that is so, elephants are not controlled by any natural predator; the natural controls that bear on them are of a different order from those affecting most other species. Starvation – and the nutritional diseases associated with it – probably more than any other factor

Elephants frequently indulge in bouts of bark-stripping, using tusks and trunk for the purpose. In the Tsavo National Park and elsewhere, the gigantic baobab trees appear to have been singled out for special attention.

Overleaf: The massive wall of the Ngorongoro Crater forms an appropriate background to these elephants and their attendant egrets.

exercises the most direct control over elephant populations.

The extent of the Tsavo problem was not appreciated until a reliable census was taken of the elephant population. The first attempt, made in October 1957, recorded 2,639 elephants in an area covering about 20 per cent of the park. As most of the herds were thought to be in this particular sector of the park at the time, it was assumed that the entire park population was about 3,000 elephants.

Imagine, therefore, the surprise when the first full-scale aerial census, undertaken in 1965, showed that there were 15,678 elephants in the park. By 1969, this figure had risen to the phenomenal total of more than 20,000, with a further 10–12,000 estimated to inhabit the areas adjoining the park's eastern boundary which, in contrast with the westerly side of the park, was not subject to

intensive human pressures.

Viewed against these figures – infinitely higher than anyone at the time thought possible – the elephant seemed almost overnight to have changed from an animal in desperate need of protection from poachers to a sinister menace bent on the destruction of Kenya's largest national park. By their destruction of trees, the elephants have profoundly altered the vegetation of the park from *Commiphera-Acacia* woodland to predominantly open grassland. The implications of this fundamental change are far-reaching, not only for the elephant itself but for the entire complex of species in and around the park.

Conversion of the Tsavo National Park's woodland to perennial grassland means that the habitat available to the grazing animals is increased at the expense of the browsing

animals. Thus, there is a change from bush-dependent species, to grass-dependent species. The number of giraffe, lesser kudu, dikdik and other browsers declines, while the grazing species, such as the gazelles, buffalo, zebra and oryx, increase. The bird population is, of course, also affected, the rich and diverse woodland bird fauna being replaced by the fewer and less varied grassland bird species.

Thus the character of Tsavo has altered dramatically. Whether that change is for better or worse is a question that defies rational reply, for either way the answer is meaningless. We can be sure of only one thing: Nature is in process of continual change, much of it barely perceptible but occasionally punctuated by violent convulsions. The events that have taken place at Tsavo are an integral part of that process

in which flood, drought and fire have played their part. The deaths of 5,000 elephants (one quarter of the park's total elephant population) in the 1970–71 drought, as well as the great increase in the numbers of plains game are some of the more obvious factors contributing to the striking of a new balance – part of the never-ending cycle of change.

The fundamental question raised by these events is the extent to which interference in this process of natural change is either desirable or justified, more especially within a national park which is ecologically incomplete. Should a national park, in other words, be managed in conformity with preconceived notions of what the natural balance should be or should there be no interference with the cyclic processes?

Until about twenty years ago very little reliable knowledge existed about the natural

**Left: From the verandah of Kenya's Tree Tops Hotel visitors have a spectacular view of a herd of elephants at close quarters.**

**Above: A boat provides the most convenient platform for viewing elephants in Uganda's Murchison Falls National Park.**

history and the ecology of the animals we were aiming to conserve. Then in the 1950s a series of ecological and behavioural studies were made which, with gathering momentum, have done much to provide the kind of evidence that is basic to the future of the national parks and the wildlife they were established to perpetuate.

With wild animals being increasingly restricted to artificially contrived sanctuaries by barriers of settlement and cultivation, the current need is for greater understanding of such matters as nutrition and stress, two crucially important subjects about which little is at present known but which are bound to assume greater significance in the future.

Urgent consideration also needs to be given to the effects of tourism. At what point does tourism itself become detrimental to the well-being of a national park? With governments attempting to squeeze every possible economic advantage from tourism, there is a strong possibility of some national parks becoming so tourist-orientated that they will come more and more to resemble glorified zoos.

We need to be constantly reminded of Professor E. W. Russell's definition of a national park as 'an area set aside where man can enjoy, as a privileged visitor, the plants and animals that are indigenous to that environment under conditions as little affected by his presence as possible, and the Trustees of a Park hold it in trust for the benefit of future generations as well as for the present'.

Nowhere is the problem of confinement to sanctuaries more acute than in Sri Lanka, formerly Ceylon. The Ceylon elephant at one time roamed widely over the island, but is now largely confined to three national parks, each more or less isolated from the other: Ruhuna in the south-west Wilpattu in the north-east, and Gal Oya in the east.

Although these reserves were established specifically for the protection of the elephant, both Gal Oya and Ruhuna are in the drier part of the island and are therefore unable to sustain the herds throughout the year. Early in the dry season shortage of food forces the elephants out of the parks for a period of three or four months. In other words, for about one-third of each year they are obliged to leave the protected areas.

Many of the trails followed by the elephants as they move about the island have been used for generations. Peasant cultivation, at first limited to the lowlands, later spread into the highlands, following the introduction first of coffee then of tea. The establishment of plantations and intensive development of the highlands interrupted the elephants' trek routes, thereby cutting them off from their traditional dry-season foraging areas in the upland forests.

Despite being legally protected in Sri Lanka, the elephant can of course be shot in defence of life and property. The animal's habit of wandering and its inability to resist the temptation of raiding sugar plantations and standing crops brings it into conflict with man. As trespassing elephants can inflict enormous damage in the course of a single night, many are shot in the interests of crop protection.

Crop damage by elephants is a long-standing problem. In 1831, when the island's elephant population was estimated to number about 12,000, the damage grew so serious that the government encouraged their reduction by means of a bounty scheme, ten shillings being paid for every elephant killed. The inducement was evidently sufficient to force the government to lower the rate to seven shillings, for, as Sir Samuel Baker tells us, 'the number killed was so great that the Government imagine that they cannot afford the annual outlay'. An indication of the number killed can be gained from the tally of 1400 elephants killed by one celebrated hunter of the period alone.

As agricultural development takes in more and more of the Sri Lanka highlands, the survival of the elephant becomes increasingly dependent upon the national parks. But the existing national parks are inadequate for the purpose. Unless the system of parks can be improved to meet the elephant's full ecological requirements, thereby enabling the herds to remain under protection throughout the year, the future for the Ceylon elephant must be bleak.

This is not simply a matter of boundary adjustment. The work of the Smithsonian Elephant Survey has shown the need for managing the buffalo in the interests of the elephant. Since the establishment of the Yala National Park, the number of buffalo–

previously kept down by hunting–has increased under protection until their numbers are now excessive: they consume so much of the available plant food that insufficient remains for the elephants which are then forced to seek food elsewhere.

In addition to the 2150 wild elephants in Ceylon, there are a further 7,500 in India. Borneo is estimated to have 2,000, Thailand a mere 500. As there are no reliable estimates for Burma or any of the other South-East Asian countries in which wild elephants occur, it is impossible to make an accurate assessment of the overall total.

But the general trend is probably not very different from Sumatra where, if the situation in the northern province of Azeh typifies the island as a whole, the elephant is clearly in serious decline. A survey undertaken by the Nature Protection and Wildlife Management Service in 1970 shows that during the last 30–40 years the number of elephants has declined by about two-thirds: there are now fewer than 100 elephants in the entire province. The survivors have been reduced to remnant herds often cut off from each other by the spread of agriculture.

Perhaps the best hope for safeguarding the Sumatran elephant, as the Service itself proposes, would be to revive the system of training elephants for domestic purposes. At one time, retinues of domesticated elephants were maintained by the country's rulers, but early in the nineteenth century this practice was abandoned. Its revival would provide the incentive to maintain some of the wild herds, if only to supply domestic replacements. At present there is no such inducement, with the result that, despite nominal protection, the elephant is regarded not only as 'useless' but actually a menace to orderly development.

A comparatively new threat to the elephant in India has come from the widespread use of agricultural pesticides to destroy wildlife. Since the mid-1950s, pesticides–notably endrine and folidol–have been used in India for the destruction of tigers, leopards and other predators. Folidol, which is both odourless and tasteless, is freely distributed by the Indian Department of Agriculture. Its indiscriminate use has been an important factor in the drastic reduction of the Bengal tiger; it is now being increasingly used to kill elephants. In the Indian state of Kerala, for example, the carcasses of 38 elephants were found in one six-month period; most had died from poisoning. Pesticides are sprayed around the edge of cultivated land and bunches of treated bananas are left on elephant trails.

As forests are felled to make way for expanding agriculture, the future of the Asiatic elephant becomes increasingly dependent on the existing mosaic of national parks and reserves. All the evidence points to the inadequacy of the present systems of reserves: unless measures can be taken to improve them, the time will come when the only remaining wild Asiatic elephants will be those inhabiting the few, unspoiled natural areas that are too remote or otherwise unsuitable to be taken over by peasant agriculturalists. Even that modest aim is a receding hope. For how do you rate the chances of there being any land available for future elephants in the face of the human earthquake which in India alone has increased the population from 270 to 530 millions in the past 35 years?

Left: Wild Asiatic elephants are comparatively difficult to see in the wild, partly because of their growing scarcity and partly because of the denseness of their chosen habitat.

Below: A wild Asiatic elephant enjoying its daily bath.

Bottom: Elephants are very much at home in water and are competent swimmers. This herd of Asiatic elephants has just waded across a wide river.

# INDEX

*Page numbers in italics indicate illustrations*

95

## Acknowledgments

*The publishers would like to thank the following organizations and individuals for their kind permission to reproduce the photographs in this book:*

Heather Angel 82–3, 84; Ardea 56–7, (Su Gooders) 30, (Su Gooders/W. E. G. Foyle) 70 above, (Clem Haagner) 33, 39 right, 53, 94, (P. Morris) 7; Bavaria-Verlag (B. Leidmann) 37, 45, (Strobel) 35; Camerapix 42 below, 44; Bruce Coleman (Des Bartlett) 27, 90–91, (D. and J. Bartlett) 40–41, (Mark N. Boulton) 16, (Norman Myers) 78, (G. D. Plage) 21 above, (Masud Quarishy) 49, (Alan Root) 43, (Simon Trevor) endpapers, 13, 21 below; Cooper-Bridgeman 71; Gerald Cubitt 87 above right; Mary Evans Picture Library 10, 11, 66, 76–7, 77 left, 77 right, 77 below right, 80; Virginia Fass 62, 62–3; Michael Holford 75, (Victoria and Albert Museum) 60 right; Eric Hosking 28–9, 32, 86–7; Alan Hutchison 4–5, 17, 54–5, 68, 69 above, 74–5; Jacana (Alain Antony) 38–9, (Eliott) 52 below, (V. Renaud) 24–5, 46, (Robert) 14, 26 below, 52 above, (A. Visage) 12–13, 42 above, (Walker) 15; David Keith Jones 23; Paolo Koch 1, 2–3, 22, 58, 59 below, 64–5, 65, 79, 84–5, 91; Frank Lane 47, 50, (F. Hartmann) 50–51; Natural Science Photos (Isobel Bennett) 36–7, 83, (Richard Kemp) 88–9, (photo G. Kinns, model A. Hayward) 6–7; NHPA (Douglas Dickens) 26 above, (J. Good) 20, (Peter Johnson) 30, (E. H. Rao) 92–3 below, 93 right; Salmer (J. Allan Cash) 68–9; Scala 61; F. & N. Schwitter Photographic Library (Rolf-Jürgen Wagner) 28; Tierbilder Okapia 17, 48 above, 72–3; Victoria and Albert Museum 81; Elizabeth Weiland 70 below; World Wildlife Fund (E. P. Gee) 92–3 above; ZEFA (E. Bleicher) 67 below, (Dr. Klaus Bonath) 59 above, 87 below right, (H. Helmlinger) 18–19, (Leidmann) 30–31, 60 left, (E. Mariani) 55, (K. Röhrich) 67 above.